Freeflow Books
Copyright ©2014
ISBN: 978-149 4709655
Library of Congress Catalog Card Number: Geez, I can't even get my local librarian to shelve my books. What makes you think I got any chance with the Feds?

The paintings are property of the author, who would very much like to make them someone else's property.

Author will clean your property, or cook on it for those of you better suited to making money than author seems to be. He will wipe the floor and wall behind the couch and bake his signature dish, *Umami Macaroni and Cheese*, for less an hour than what you paid for this book. I need to slip into the economy just a little bit. Work under the table, that sort of thing. I can't be bound by a manager's time schedule. There's too much going on here at home.

Cover design by Ron and Rose Throop (mostly Rose).

I have kept a blog for seven years running. The name has changed from time to time. There are rests, usually in summer, when the mind is set in "gather ye rosebuds while ye may" mode. Then I shy away from the computer. By May the focus shifts and I seek communion with nature, more or less, keeping my mental distance away from the hydra-headed problems of mankind.

I think this technology has been either my wealth or my ruin in matters of career. Time will tell. Presently I don't think I have one reader beyond my closest friends. Even posting links to the blog on Facebook (where I enjoy the friendship of 23 bosom buddies) just echoes the song of crickets in the human-made cavernous void I enter whenever I seek an advocate of the same species.

Still, Google has improved my channels for expression a thousandfold. Unfortunately for the artist-entrepreneur every one else is wired too. The playing field is leveled. The information is on overload. I cannot ask a question without a friend or family member checking for the answer on a smartphone. Yesterday my sister and mother were coming up with anagrams. Short ones. Like *Bob*, *mom*, and *boob*. Then I had my wife look up the longest anagram on line. Turns out that my sister and mother were making palindromes, not anagrams, and the longest is *detartrated*. So much for anyone having a mind of their own anymore. We're all so freaking digitally smart!

This would be okay with me if these queries were limited to choosing the most potent antibiotic, or the right direction after "I think I made a wrong turn in Albuquerque. Siri, please advise". They are not. Already I cannot sit through a sought after dumbed-down poker game without half of my friends verifying their beer queries with iPhone research. Soon enough, no one will share any worthwhile knowledge or opinion without "officially" checking first. Better be able to back up your claim grandma that the sky is falling. Cite Google Earth. Otherwise, "Ow! I just got hit on the head!"

Anyway, my blog has been a Google Blog at address: www.tamandfriends.blogspot.com. But I am moving on to Wordpress. Open source. Less greed for my need.

http://throop4.wordpress.com/

Blogging is free for me and no advertising to you. I write and paint what I want, and sometimes even refuse to check my sources with the librarian Internet. Blasphemy!

Also, I rarely open a comment thread to allow for rebuttal, for if one truly cared so much about a subject that I care about, then I expect a postage-stamped letter, or at least a reaction posted on his or her own blog or website. My job is expression, not debate. Still, as I said before, I have few if any readers. I need to connect traditionally. Google is a fine notetaker, but I cannot trust my creativity to the eternal care of a corporate cloud. Hence the following publication.

Recently I have used several spamming devices to gain attention *Internetedly*. I used Twitter to profile people who might be interested and sent them a link in 140 carefully arranged characters or less. Unfortunately it just made a lot of tweeters mad, and I got sent to the principal's office on several occasions.

That certainly didn't get me any frequent return visits to my blog either. So although the Internet is very good as venue to show the angst out of yourself, it breeds a kind of insanity to the expressionist if nobody participates. I am provided my own private padded room with straight-jacket. I can paint while chomping on a paintbrush, but if the warden doesn't want my pictures to leave the silly cell, they never will.

So, I return to traditional means. The printed word. I have applied my craft to both mediums. This one is better. Here one can feel, archive, and then walk away. Books contain tomorrow's histories, while the Internet complains of a head cold today.

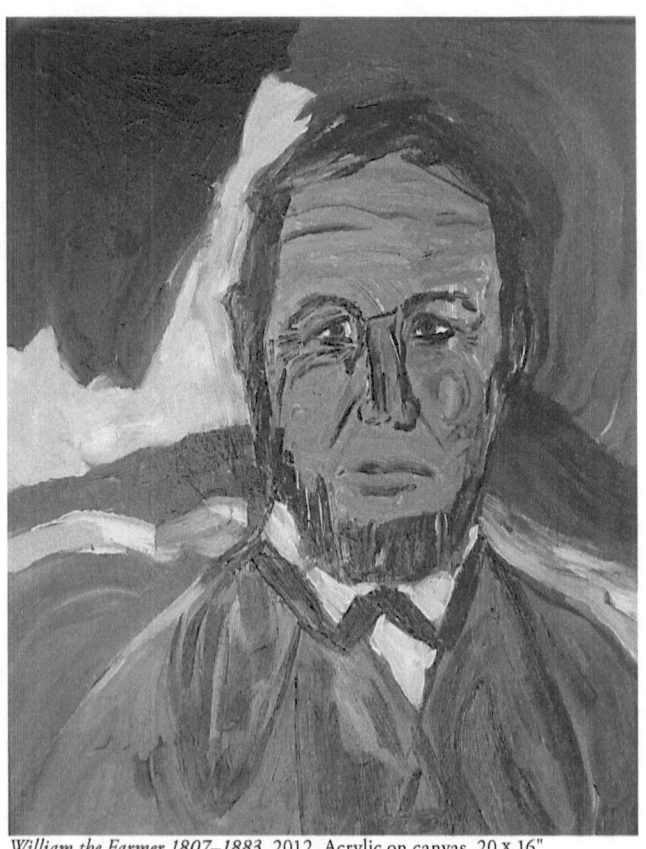

William the Farmer 1807–1883. 2012. Acrylic on canvas, 20 × 16"

Living Dog, Dead Lion

With freedoms taken two centuries ago by hungry families, and not by modern soldiers plying their government paid racket in Europe, Africa and Asia, comfort and joy are now ours for the seeking. We have prosperity and well-funded public libraries for the free exchange of ideas. The philanthropist social reformer Gerrit Smith funded our city library in 1853. He made two demands; locate the library on the east side of the Oswego River, and shut out no person on account of race, complexion, or condition, even if you think he or she looks like a fervent child predator (italics mine).

Last winter the library director broke Mr. Smith's bylaw. She followed me around the children's room eager to catch an act of supreme perversion. I was finished collecting books and magazines for the school week (we homeschooled), and my daughter Sophie looked over her picks while I stood beside her at the tall windows, staring out at the winter sky to daydream. After a while the director peeked around a shelf and asked if she could help me.

"No thank you. I'm just looking at the view."

Then she asked again, but with a little more strain in her voice.

"Sir, can I help you?"

"No."

Pause. She stared at me nonplussed. Suddenly the "flight or fight" nerves jumped circus leaps across my skin.

"Ma'am, you're scaring me," I said.

"You're scaring the children," she replied, and glanced at Sophie seated to her right, insinuating that I made a visit to the library today to abduct, flash or fornicate with junior scholars. I wasn't the only parent there. It was furlough week at the school prison, and moms and dads were all about the place, frantic in their inexperience with pedagogy.

I looked around in complete disbelief. My hair was cut, my face clean-shaven; I wore a gray London Fog overcoat circa 1966—Oh!

So, the $80,000/year library director was profiling potential perversion by my poor choice of winter wear in a children's library, even if I wasn't staring at the kids with a pronounced tongue loll. Then I remembered how she approached me earlier, while I flipped through the kid's periodicals, looking for science articles to read with Sophie.

"Can I help you?"

"No thank you," I said. "I like to find things out by myself. It's more fun."

That line must have sounded a siren in her brain. One eye was probably glued on me for the next fifteen minutes while her imagination played out disgusting scenarios in her perverted mind.

My thrice great-grandfather William Throop knew Gerrit Smith personally. I have letters he wrote confirming their relationship. William and Gerrit shook hands at lectures and meetings, and perhaps even discussed the unwarranted exclusion of perverts and pedophiles in public institutions. What a remarkable sea change of society to be an accused clean-shaven 21st century man in his forties leaning against a mid-nineteenth century window sill. The fear bomb is ticking inside each one of us, even the professional public officials who deal with the good and bad of a city every day, and should know from experience all the makes and models of its social dregs. Still, some big irrationality informed the librarian that I was a threat to her charges. She felt the need to confront and accuse me without any revealed outward indication except that I appeared dangerous in her mind. The sad truth is that after clearing up my innocence (pointing out that Sophie was my daughter), I reminded the director that our family posed for a photography session in her living room just a few years prior. She told me I should understand that this is a dangerous world and she needs to be on the lookout for the children's sake. Needless to say I was shaking with confusion and disbelief for the remainder of the day. I have always walked proud with my daughters, yet that afternoon I felt that I looked to everyone else like a stalking child molester in my chosen neighborhood.

Gerrit Smith poses for a photo in his old age. Sure, he looks the part of a typical 19th century child-toucher. No doubt that if alive today, as soon as he sat that long gray beard and fat round ass down on a chair at the children's library, our director would call the police. Even if he admonished her with some words of reminder that it was his legacy which promoted the right of any man or woman, light or dark, socially sane or insane to become a library director. Distrust and cowardice is the new black in the American psychology. Five generations have passed since admirable human pride has digressed to a stone-age knee-jerk reactionary fear of everything we cannot control. So watch your backs fathers of Oswego! Keep away from your own spawn, especially if taking on any kind of interest in their intellectual development. Best to stay uninformed and working those fingers hard to callous. Remember to wash your hands in motor oil before coming to the library. The director will look to see the grease in your pores. She wants to check your threat by Oswego man standards. The only men who come to the children's room are fathers who look very uncomfortable standing in the center of it. The director imagines a draft beer or monkey wrench grasped in each hand before determining a threat level. Come there erect and proud and you might be judged a pervert. See? I said, "erect". It can't be helped. Onto the pink bean bags fellow predators of my town and country! We'll lean back, grin, and rub our hands together to the tender morsels all around.

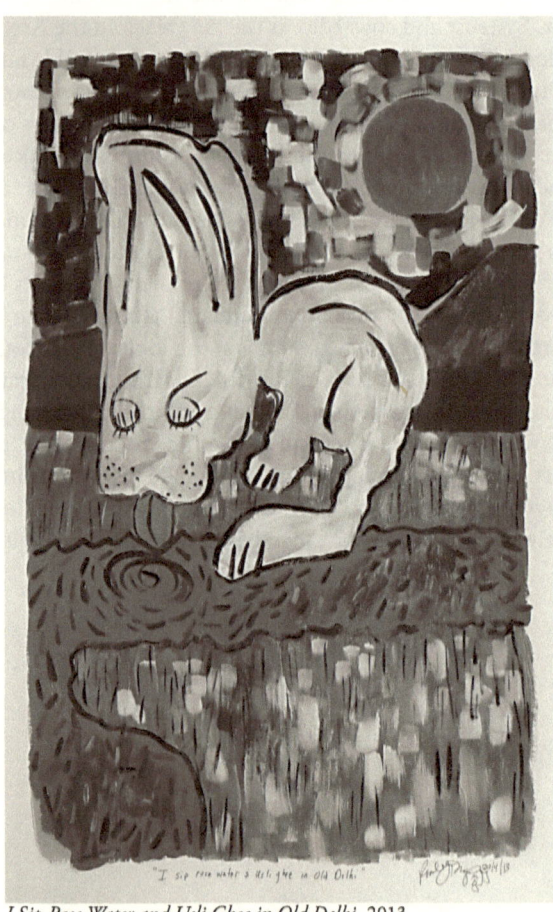

I Sip Rose Water and Usli Ghee in Old Delhi. 2013.
Acrylic on paper, 22 x 15"

Christie's Fall Auction Meets the Wastelander Gauge™

While driving down the highway yesterday en route to visit family, my wife and I engaged in the usual discussion about the "why"
of art. I told her that this week I intend to haul the present contents
of Christie's auction house over to the county dump. I have rented
a refuse stall next to recycling so the wet smells will be tolerable
for my afternoon of auctioneering. The whole lot is ready for quick
sale. A few of Jean-Michel Basquiat's 16-minute paintings, 2 Cindy
Sherman photographs of a stranger, and a de-Kooning charcoal of
any B.F.A.'s skill and ability, to name a few. I am excited about my
chances here in small town upstate New York. Especially if I make
bidding begin on Saturday morning, when the trucks line up a
quarter-mile to drop off trash proof of their incredible bad taste.

I will start with Cindy's photograph of the face of a girl who
looks frightened. My beautiful assistant, Rose (who by the way,
is also an emerging photographer) will hold the picture up while
walking the line of Ford F350's. "Photo of a young girl who looks
scared. Can I get a dollar?"

A low diesel growl up and down the line. Country radio stations
playing. Then finally a bearded man in a rusty Toyota calls Rose
over to his window.

"I'll give ya a dollar."

"All right," she calls, "I have a dollar. Do I hear a dollar fifty?"
Diesel growl.

"Going once, twice... Sold to the white trash in the red Toyota."

The Cindy Sherman envelope gets thirty-three cents dropped
in to it. The Throops keep the rest for their business savvy and
distribution prowess.

Next on the block is Basquiat's *Blue Heads*. This is a big one,
and while moving it across the road, the painting gets awkwardly
wedged in between two trucks. Traffic gets stopped and the horns
sound off. It starts to rain. A couple dudes get out of their cabs to
help me out. Pull and push, push and pull. Suddenly, Jean-Michel's
masterpiece breaks in half and falls face down in the muddy slop.
Still, we manage to get $25 for the frame from some guy building a
sub floor in his laundry room.

$8.33 into Jean-Michel's estate envelope.

De-Kooning's charcoal gets no buyers, and unfortunately we forgo Jeff Koons' pink poodle because the dump officer says we'll have to pay a fee on the weight, and there's no way we can front the cost on that kind of establishment crap.

After a full day of selling contemporary art at the dump, the staff of Throop Auction House is able to pay for dinner and tip at the Ritz Diner downtown. I got an omelet. Rose ordered the macaroni and cheese. And the bubble building faux-artists of earth got just what they deserve: a meal to fuel the next inspiration.

So this week I will do my darnedest to burst the bubble of the visual art market and the artists who blow it up with hot, hot air, enabling the radical class, earth's multi-millionbillionaires, to inflate human creativity like tulip bulbs in Amsterdam. Their art collection has real value worth a decent used car, and yet they continue to play the game of sell and resell, because we of the creative class, the village idiots and dreamers, keep hoping that our time will come. It won't. It won't ever. We have been relegated to the dung heap by the no-class class of wasters. If you wanted to get into their club, and aren't by now, then you never ever will be invited.

So join me. What have you got to lose? Your fifty dollar prize at the art association? Your pipe dream of being introduced by the community college president? I want David Geffen to wake up tomorrow and be informed that the Cindy Sherman photo he bought tonight for $989,000.00 has been reappraised for a hundred bucks, but only because of its mahogany frame. That's all it was ever worth anyway. And that phony cheese Sherman knows it too.

So come back each morning this week to read my reviews of this autumn's select pieces at Christie's. I will also provide fresh ideas for a better, more accessible art market of the future. But most importantly by the end of the week, every single moron millionaire will have his or her collection reduced to a rational value. I will use my wastelander gauge™ to appraise works of contemporary art. An unnamed tween subsisting on a daily meal of millet and salt, but who otherwise maintains a gentle disposition and hopeful outlook, will mark each piece at her village's fair market value. That is, the art is priced at whatever the tribal leader would pay for it. My professional guess is that the Cindy Sherman won't be worth a stick for the cooking pit. And the charcoal piece by a drunken de Kooning looks to any village elder like the bottom of the cooking pit before the morning fire. Not even the most sophisticated leader would waste a grunt nor head nod to acquire that for his wife's mud room decor.

Just in case the Sherman photo bombs, here is one of Rose's. It's called, "Holy Cow, at Least It's Not Another Rancid Slab of Hog Meat for Millionaires to Play Catch With".

Or otherwise known as *Flower in Hand*.

Fifty bucks.

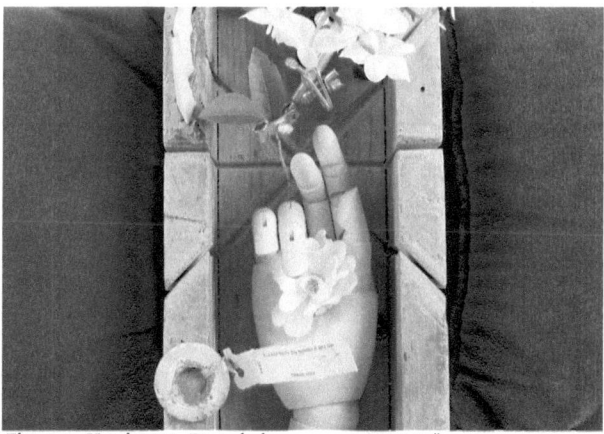

Flower in Hand. 2013. Digital photo on paper, 8 ˟ 10"

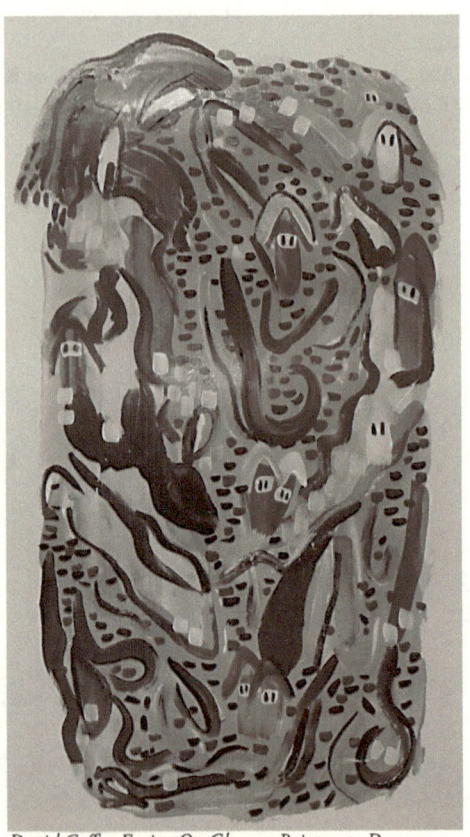

David Geffen Egging On Ghanan Painters to Drown Themselves in Lake Volta. 2013.
Acrylic on paper, 17 x 10"

David Geffen Cannot Afford Me

Here is a painting meeting the deadline for Christie's line-up tonight at auction. I was barely given notice, reseiving the request at dinner and tasked with a proofed image by midnight. Still, I remained steadfast, kept sober, and while painting, found the time to cook dinner, wash the dishes, sift the cat litter, help my daughter with math homework, listen to her presentation on aerobic respiration, and joke with her about boys. Phew!

Anyway, Christie's called this morning and asked me to set up last night's painting on-line—by request of their eBay pal Pierre Omidyar. He wants in on this high-end poker game of art. Well, I won't argue. I need Christies because America says I can be a millionaire too, just once before I die.

I listed on eBay: David Geffen Egging On Ghanan Painters to Drown Themselves in Lake Volta. No reserve bid either. I am told that the billionaires will be scouting this one tonight. Especially Eli Broad, who would love to get one more jab at that "flighty Geffen" and win a high bid. They say my piece competes on a level with photographs by Cindy Sherman. The timing is right. Most of the billionaire sex perverts are tired of buying up her feminist politics.

Christie's provides a prerecorded explanation of her piece on their website. They deliver better than God could if promised a 40% cut of the predicted million bucks. Those consummate Christie's pros know right where to put the cotton in the nasal passage of the narrator too, to give his voice that special "you want to believe I am not screwing you, but know of course that I am, and with a large pipe" sound.

The Cindy Sherman entry at Chritie's: *Untitled #92.* Assessed (by whom?) between 900K and 1.2 million American dollars. Here is my criticism, as deep as time will allow:

Ready?

It is what it is.

This means that every student of art history who makes a postgrad living authenticating charlatans like Sherman needs these silly schoolyard billionaires more than air and not much less than water. An iron lung could keep them breathing, but liquids need to flow. Without David Geffen's complete worship of abstract money, abstract power, and more abstract money and power, all enablers are reduced to the likes of me and my comrades, the struggling Ghanan painters. In my painting (above and in grayscale unfortunately) you can see them drowning in Lake Volta, where Christie's, Cindy Sherman, David Geffen, and Eli Broad have poured in enough acid avarice to toxify the lake and burn the skin off them while sinking. They laugh, laugh, laugh while artists of every society, metaphorically flail and fall alone, grasping to futile hopes of saving themselves. No longer are there comrades of art getting together in cafes to discuss the brutality of Imperialism, the wonder of color, the joy of living. No more George Grosz type, dressing up like a wealthy industrialist loathing the upper class with a mad bitterness that infects his consumptive friends with born again, youthful vitality, and a playful desire to piss on the money hoarders.

Today, posers like Banksy post money-making ideas on Instagram, to tease stupid billionaires with clever genius (and get rich while doing it). Self-made? Hardly. A dues paying member of the working class artist guild? In his dreams. Rather just another air conditioned Caucasian puppet man entertaining the boredom of boring billionaires.

So the Cindy Sherman photograph... What is its true worth? Well, a good marker would be for Cindy to enter her piece into the Lakeside Statewide Juried Art Exhibition this spring at the Oswego Art Association. She needs to send in a digital image by early February, and there is no guarantee of acceptance into the gallery. But if she's lucky, I mean really lucky (for no photograph has ever won Best of Show), she will take home a $300 cash award and get a write-up in the local shopper. She can set an asking price of $900,000, and Bill the gallery director will dutifully mark it, (a few visitors on opening night will assume she's just "pulling a Ron Throop" who usually does the opposite and sets a ridiculously low price for inspired work). Her tastefully framed photograph will hang there nearly thermostatically controlled while Oswego's final winter winds blow, blow, and blowwww. Sadly, no one at the art association can afford her creepy "girl before she gets ravaged" photograph. There aren't any billionaires in town. Last year our first multimillionaire broke a world record doing chin-ups in his weight room. So there isn't any taste in Oswego either. Her best bet at that price is to seek an exclusive non-existent agent to the Fortune 500 players and cross her fingers. More likely, she can pick it up in April and begin dreaming of herself as an accomplished local arteest.

Christie's expects a million dollars for a photograph.
I can hear the grisly screams from Ghanan painters.
And you may begin bidding on the my piece... Now!

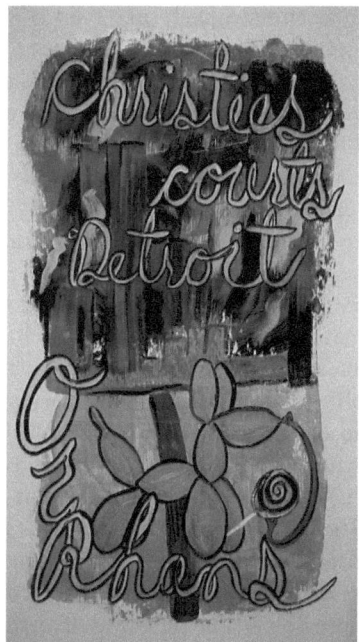

Christie's Courts Detroit Orphans. 2013.
Acrylic on paper, 15 x 8"

Christie's Courts Detroit Orphans

Day after November 2013 Contemporary Art Auction at Christie's in which Jeff Koons' Orange Balloon Dog is Bought By Billionaire Bob

There you have it! Now every published college level primer on art history has our Nero American art embarrassment to drill into the blockheads of Christie's next generation of art history PhD's. $58,400,000.00. Congratulations to the poodle's buyer. You are now, in the majority opinion of card-carrying art association members across America, a ranky stank piece of walking garbage. You have supplied a sexual deviant designer and his genteel pimps with wealth forever and beyond. Ha-ha. Or so you think. My wife and I snuck a Detroit orphan up through the belly of that Trojan Poodle a few nights ago. He holds a set of keys, one for the trap door and the other starts the engine to the last proud memory of Detroit—an immaculately preserved 1976 Cadillac Coupe Deville. The orphan we chose has a tendency for wild, flailing fits when he doesn't get what he wants. He didn't want one man to make this much money from a roomful of bidders for billionaires. Not while his city was falling apart. The orphans and the homeless are now sharing the same soup line for purposes of consolidation. The city is broke. The soup is mystery broth. And presently Billionaire Bob, your poodle is getting scratched up good and proper by an angry poor boy.

In the accompanying painting, which you can bid on at Christie's side auction, I gave the balloon poodle a big lollipop to lick. He's courting Detroit's orphans to come live on his luxurious estate of pornographic wishes and cocaine-at-the bar dreams because orphans are all Detroit will have left to offer after a couple more of these "kick the poor where it hurts" auctions. Do you see it's long snake tongue? Detroit knows it's licked. But unfortunately for Billionaire Bob, he believes a broken city doesn't really mind getting licked again, and again. Or else he thinks they're too stupid to mind, or too busy diving at his loose change crumbs to mind. I know that Billionaire Bob just bought himself an orange oracle poodle, and the future looks shiny bright.

For the time being. Billionaire Bob might want to hire the skill of a modern Frank Lloyd Wright to build the next bullet-proof compound. Or an army of haute designers for a maximum security prison-house studded with rubies to disguise thirty foot thick walls and high curly barbed wire, not so much to keep him from escaping, but to prevent the mob mutilation of Bob and his orange attack poodle.

You know, the one he paid $58,400,000.00 for.

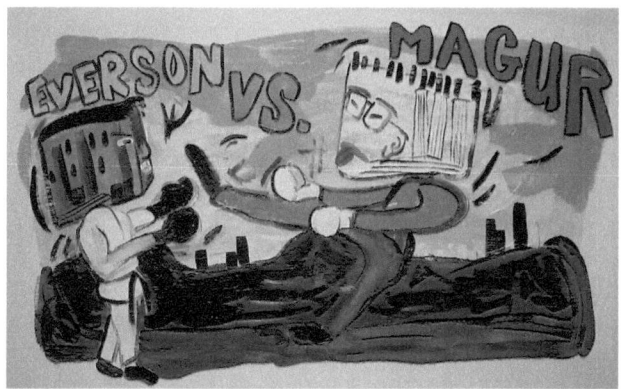

Everson Vs. Magur. 2013. Acrylic on paper, 7 x 15"

The Everson vs. The Memorial Art Gallery

Two objectives today. First individual. Second communal. In the second I fix museums. In the first I battle despair.

I am weary of thinking. S.A.D. covers me like a fog at this time of year. S.A.D. with financial worry is a toxic cloud sizzling acid into my frontal lobe.

Depression? I don't think so. It is what any man, of any culture, of any time feels when he possesses creative energy and spunk but has no waiting outlet for his expression.

"Keep it to yourself for six months mister, then in spring we'll be committed to the same routine, and not have time for you then, either."

Lows like this always bring me back to Henry Miller. He is the artist whose legacy champions the driven failure. He is the dreamer's Jesus, and *Tropic of Cancer* the New Testament. Forty-four year old man coughing up green gobs in a Paris artist ghetto delivers pure hope to the future neurotics inhabiting modern earth. Nihilism with warm bread and salted butter. Joy as a routine of failure. Happiness with no expectations. Scratch that... At least one expectation... Dinner!

Most houses of present day claiming to represent the artist are supermarket chains stocking their shelves with glossy Keebler® products. They have lost sight of the man and woman as artist. "Give us the output that PBS wants to see. We don't care about your thoughts. As long as you supply us our boxed Toll House® cookie crackers—stale or fresh, it doesn't matter. And you better dress well. And be approachable. And portfolio a resume that looks corporate like accounting..."

Oh Jesus, Henry, they're taking away art's right to failure, to jugs of wine, to 3 a.m. coffee, wild plans for the future, close friendship, and sleep as a favorite pastime for lovers. They are accomplishing the death of art in the cruelest manner to the artist. With silence! With form letters. With business. With pedaling works door-to-door, alone, in a car. Individuality and avarice. Now artists tap in like cable TV to a corporate model for communication. Twitter. Facebook. They've gone public. Promoters, promotees, a sculptor I barely know telling me in a sports bar how his friend needs to show more in order to build his resume—

These are weapons wielded by the enemies of art. Soldiers paid by anti-creative institutions. Bootlickers of art history PhD's. The temporary gatekeepers. Empty and irrelevant. Thank you Jesus Miller. Again.

Now to keep to my subject promise of finding creative ways to slaughter the corporate model that has usurped art in America.

Christie's is a pig sty, and the people who work there are rats who feed on pig drippings.

The Everson Museum is a Syracuse treasure, as is the Memorial Art Gallery of Rochester. But they have lost their way. They are mirroring their favorite soda brand ("pop" in Rochester), seeking identity in a sea of exactly the same thing museums. Each a division of Keebler trying to outdo its sister product with the "individuality" of whatever a cool million can purchase this year for the collection. Brand identity. The new thing. Like the new normalcy of networking. Concepts verbatim from page 2 in the corporate charter.

We smell a rat.

There must be three hundred or more museums of equal size

across America. And they all cry poverty in the sense that attendance is down, upkeep is up, and it just feels like so few are interested in the arts these days. The Cincinnati Art Museum spends 1.8 million on an 18 x 24" Georgia O'Keeffe and Johnny's mother is opening up a can of SpaghettiOs for breakfast so his stomach won't rumble at school today. Johnny likes the Cincinnati Bengals but the Bengals corporation wants to whore their "anything they can" on Johnny. So Johnny gets a Bengal helmet for Christmas this year. The Bengal business model was a success. The linebacker got three million. The art museum an O'Keeffe. Avarice can easily find its connections in Hell. Just plug into the bottom line.

So my idea is this: Bring local art to the status it has deserved since Barbara the Neanderthal iron oxided the cave wall with a horse, and shat in a dark corner. Today, museums around the world would be jonesing for a slab of that rock.

"France has a lot of 'gaul' to keep cave art in its own caves, especially when we're willing to offer thirty million per cubic yard."

All the artists in the Syracuse area, represented by the Everson Museum, can enter a yearly juried competition, like in January, when creatives are locally the most desperate. Same for the Memorial Art Gallery in Rochester. Each museum chooses ten of its favorites for the juror, who is from out of state and has no bias toward either city. She is invited to stay at a middle ground no-man's land along the I-90 corridor. Clyde, for instance. The host museum will alternate each time the two meet to fight. The juror judges the work, both staffs sort it out, and the top three out of five of the total twenty declares the winner museum. There is a show in summer at the home of the victor. And it receives more hype than a dead O'Keeffe, born and raised in Wisconsin (now famous in Ohio), ever deserved.

Local artists become the art stars of their own communities. Now the Everson can challenge Munson-Williams in Utica next year. The Memorial Art Gallery can take on Albright Knox in Buffalo. In a five year period, several cities can duke it out and declare a champion institution for that region.

So when the Jones family from California visits the Everson they will be shone a room displaying Syracuse's artist cream of the crop. I know the work will be just as inspired as any from van

Gogh, Picasso, or that internationally adored, anal retentive metal sculptor, who, by virtue of some corporate art Gnostics, sits atop the sculpture throne in America, even though he was born in Natchez and hates the snow.

An addendum

"On My Own Time" is an exhibit the Everson hosts every October. It is a show where participating businesses send the top two or three judged pieces from their employees, who all have a hobby called "art". Just to give you an idea of how screwy things are in our culture these days...

My friend, a marble sculptor who has shown at this venue the past two years, does university teaching *on his own time*. He spends hours searching for stone, dreaming the stone, cutting, carving, and sanding the stone. And he has something to say that he can never say while hobbying at his day job, which always pays him on time for work that is one part inspiration, three parts stultifying. And he is fortunate to practice the art of teaching. To receive his certificate for "doing art" even though he doesn't *need* to do art, can be a rewarding result of herculean effort. Along a similar vein, the poor janitor, who works at the same institution *on his own time*, scrubs dried vomit off of toilet seats in dormitories. His non-art is all stultifying. He is a photographer snapping photos in the bright light of day, from mountaintops in the Adirondacks. This makes him forget briefly that his culture and society expect him to pull hair out of clogged drains in order to take pictures *on his own time*, and never the other way around.

The show costs ten dollars for guests. It's catered. And my friend for his piece, which took him over a hundred and fifty hours of time to perfect, leaves with a show book and a desk top printed certificate.

Every time the Everson acquires another fifty thousand dollar piece of someone else's culture, they figuratively ram a can of SpaghettiOs down little Johnny's throat, and likewise remind the community that art is for the dead, just keep at it *on your own time*. The Everson needs our ignorance to fill its coffers. Like Walmart. Like Pepsi. Like McDonald's and the Cincinnati Bengals.

My friend the sculptor is an artist and a teacher. Everything he does is on his own time. The problem is that the thieves of our culture want to snatch pieces of what is ours for themselves.

The Everson and Memorial Art Gallery should exist because they are our community treasures. However they must wake up and throw open their doors to a new vitality. Keep the stuffy tomb rooms of historical art. They have their story. In my opinion they should be restocked with the art of dead central New Yorkers. I would want to know what a painter living on Midler or South Geddes was up against back in 1923. Looks pretty good. Yeah, yeah, Picasso was in Paris painting a gargoyle. And Woodrow Wilson harbored no regrets after slaughtering thousands of human beings. Jesus my dear Henry Miller, are they ever going to cut out this worship of dead kings?

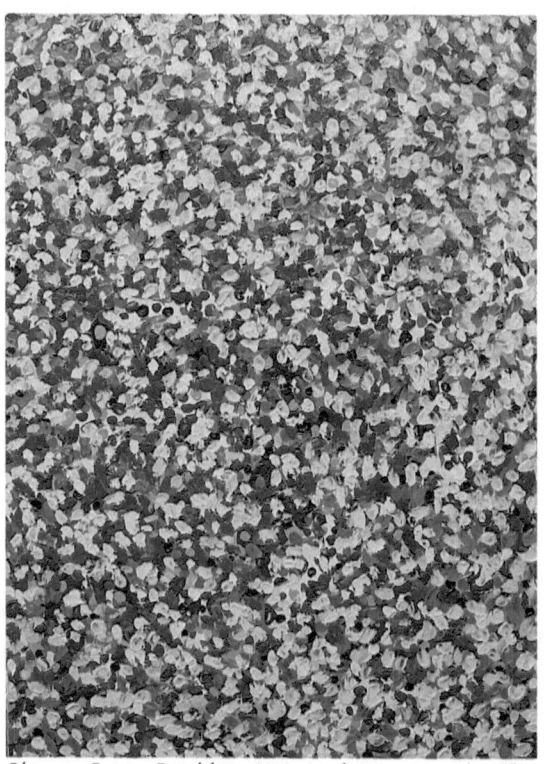

Rhiannon Beating Dandelions. 2013. Acrylic on canvas 24 x 18"

An Art Agency

Two years ago my daughter, then a senior at college and president of the student art exhibition committee, suggested that I
apply to the same agency that supplied her club with artist profiles,
from which her college regularly chose talent and invited them to
show.

So I did. It took me a full day to organize all the content request-
ed by Katherine T. Carter Associates. I was not disappointed. I got
an acceptance reply the next day. I sent in my $250.00 deposit to
secure a date to meet with Katherine in the big, big city.
Lick-lick. Check in the mail by mid-morning. Finally, after so
many years of hope and desire, and yes, action to shame an unlikely creative John Calvin, I was weeks away from representation.
Galleries! Museums! A living to be had. Modest income spawning
light travel and leisure with my wife. No longer would she need to
support me. This was a boon to the career that had not yet become
a career, through no honest fault of my own.

Then came the associates packet in the mail. The fine print. For
a total of $500.00 I would have two hours of Katherine's time to
"consult" with her. That is, listen to her pitch. For about $4,000.00
(more or less), I would have the chance to be profiled in the same
book distributed to my daughter's college, and, which I assumed,
many others to boot. No promises however. Not even an "it takes
money to make money" admittance on her part. Just $500.00 and
a two-hour talk.

Way back in 1958 my stepfather applied to be a cop in Utica, N.Y.
His cousin (already a cop) told him to give $500.00 to the city mob
boss. He walked into Mr. Falcone's pool hall and said, "Go to Hell.
I'll pass the test on my own, get the job on my own, or expose you
to the state WASP authority." Well, he must have hit a soft spot in
the heart of Mr. Mafia, because he got the job based on his ability
to work and not pay his way. And Mr. Falcone never killed him.

According to, not only Katherine Carter, but all complicit museums and galleries that deal with her, I am expected to pay my
way into this corrupt art mafia, without even being guaranteed
admittance into the elite society. I might be too political, in that

I actually make that kind of art carrying an opinion, one that is most often counter to an establishment seeking moderation in everything.

I believe that contemporary art is run by a cartel called *The Careful Family*. This is how I see it. My daughter was taught by her college how to authenticate art, to pick what the art mafia prefers. It must be good because each one of their choice professionals paid at least 1/2 a year dishwasher's salary to "get made".

Now really, who the hell is this charlatan Katherine Carter? What is she painting? Where does she get the crime boss balls to corner an industry that isn't even an industry? And to you, college and university art departments... Do you not have enough MFA's to seek what is downright good and gooey for their own students? It can be a lot of fun, actually choosing what one likes, and not what some greedy New York business person declares is likable.

I am a painter of much energy. On a spiritual level, it is enough for me to know this. Practically I have dug myself a hole two ladder lengths down from Hades. But the art students don't care. It just brings proof to the claim of the "fool persisting in his folly until he becomes wise". State College Fred and Private art school Lana would "get me". Much more than they would "get" some oil painter of Assateague wild horses, or a Columbia University PhD skilled in the silhouette cut outs of slaves being whipped and raped.

How much did *they* have to pay to get in?

Well, what do souls go for these days?

For those gallerists still wanting youth to choose what is vital, ask them if my work is worthy of a room. Tell the kids that I write too. About art and living. That's interdisciplinary and no one needs to suffer a painting of the Space Shuttle to round out a course. They can see my stuff on a blog I keep, which is a week's wages worth cheaper than the phony art realty listings in the Katherine Carter Associates' book. A little push is all I need. That, and a 1/2 a year dishwasher's salary.

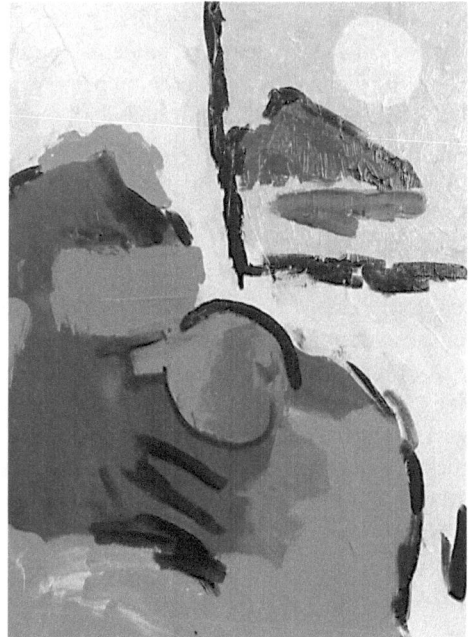

Birth of Sophia. 2013. Acrylic on canvas, 24 x 18"

Moods and Memories

This month I am trying something different. Working toward a
body of work for a future show that points to moods and mem-
ories of my past. Very meditative. Each canvas the same size
and depth (18 x 24" studio), which makes the process just lightly
unaffordable. I am always seeking a gallery that employs professionals with working eyes attached to optic nerves. That is, people
to either like or not like, without needing to be taught what to like
or not to like. No art agents or sixteen page resumes necessary to
convince gallerists and curators who graduated from university
educated and dreamy. Those to see something, like it, and then
proceed to introduce themselves and form a relationship with the
artist. Socially brave professionals. More rare than self-toasting

bread.

Yet if there is an art agent or curator out there who doesn't require ten hours of the literary forgery which is every visual artist's phony persuasive essay and cooked resume, then by all means find me and employ me. I am hyper-diligent. Put me to work. Set the price. And if you need a good story to share with the elite class, you tell them they should just see what I keep in my pocket. Or, how I attend to my toilet a step ahead of van Gogh's privy with shovel and spoon. Tell them I have murdered gently, and not only am I more gay than Sunday, but wildly interested in geckos donning used Barbie swim wear.

More likely, to the chagrin of all unknowns like myself, curators will wait for the market media to declare those artists who are up and coming, or rehash the established cash cows for the billionaires to trade.

Honestly I am amazed at how rudely even the smallest galleries have processed my queries. Biting the hand that feeds them, no doubt. Maybe I would too if all I ever got for my business was dried oil or plastic color and varying rectangles of inedible cellulose.

Oops. Already do.

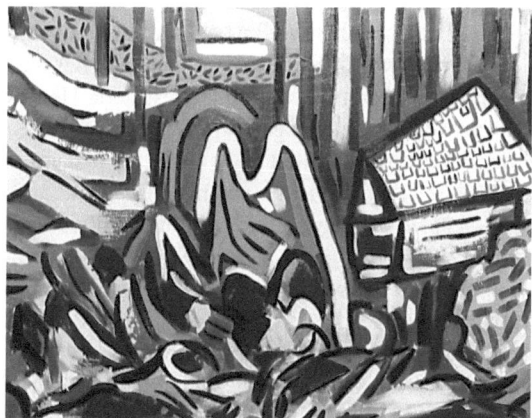

Birth of Rose. 2013. Acrylic on canvas, 18 x 24"

Bob Dylan is a Greedy Man

Bob Dylan is a dog. A wealthy one. An intelligent one. But a
dog nonetheless. For a man who has made millions on creativity,
(much deserved in the medium of songwriting), he doesn't need
a wooden nickel for his paintings, and now unfortunately we
hear, his welding. At least not while he is alive. Damn dog. Damn
monkey with a head for business. He's a monkey and a dog. Damn
greedy monkey dog who is playing the market like a pro, knowing
darn well what the brand Dylan with fetch from the millionaire
lawyers. But he paints like any painter, that is, paintably. And he
welds like any welder can weld when a welder has a maid and a
private cook. What more could he possibly need? Fill up a gallery with soft millionaire strokes and that's one less gallery for
the desperate strugglers to achieve. Oh I bet as a young man on
a slushy Soho street he waved a fist or two at the established folk
singer tools stuffing their portfolios with easy money. He got his
break at a time when suits decided to merge their distribution
talents with the creative joys of artists. Vinyl could be shelved all
over the world, like toilet paper and mayonnaise. It was win-win
for the new industry. Columbia Records could not have gambled

on a more successful poster child. For Bob was an artist, *then*. And like any artist worth his salt, he held a skyscraper chip on his shoulder for the rest of his life. He proved day after day why choosing him was a good idea, a sound investment. He worked at it. And improved. And never gave up. Why? Because he didn't have to. Lunch was always available. Dinner and a late night snack too. After 1963, he could dip in any swimming pool at any time, and there would always be a room for him while traveling, always a seat on an airplane.

Bob Dylan the man has got his piece of the pie. He is a genius, a super creative person, but he is no longer an artist. Bob Dylan the dog knows he can pretend beg in other mediums, and achieve wild success, because of fame, not struggle. He's like the old coddled poodle of a J.P. Morgan wife. He will take what he can get because he can get it. Steak on a plate, or a walk in the park. Anything he wants, because there are mindless people out there who will spoil a dog rotten. He began no more or less creative than other creative poodles in the city, but he happens to be the family poodle of one of the richest people on the planet. Beef bones will be stocked for him in perpetuity inside the Morgan tomb.

The economy of idiots is manipulated by the savvy business elite. Isn't it obvious now? Mercedes and Bob Dylan are one in the same thing, it's true. However Dylan is also a human being, and a mon-umentally greedy one at that. His paintings will sell very well for posterity, his grandchildren, his grand children's grandchildren can live in luxury because of the late twentieth centuries' wildly profitable cult of personality. But that's not enough for Bob. He wants it now. All of it now. If he pooped in a dog park, it and a ball jar might fetch a few hundred bucks on eBay, provided there were photos of the act to authenticate. Heck, in these days of light speed funny-money, it's a sure thing that a fresh Bob pile will beget at least a weekly paycheck to an unknown artist. Knowing this I think Bob will hoard a septic tank supply for his own pre-coffin coffers.

Bob Dylan. The great Midwestern welder. Miner and artist of iron ore. The working man's working man. Having the butler tip the pool cleaners, and another London gallerist turns her nose up to the eager emerging artist. Unlike Bob, his crap is not golden. It'll fetch literal shit on the market.

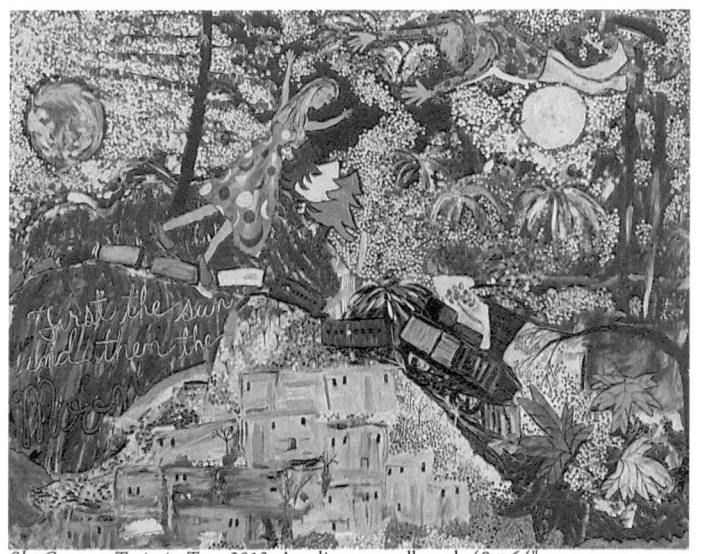

She Got on a Train in Taos. 2013. Acrylic on panelboard, 48 x 64"

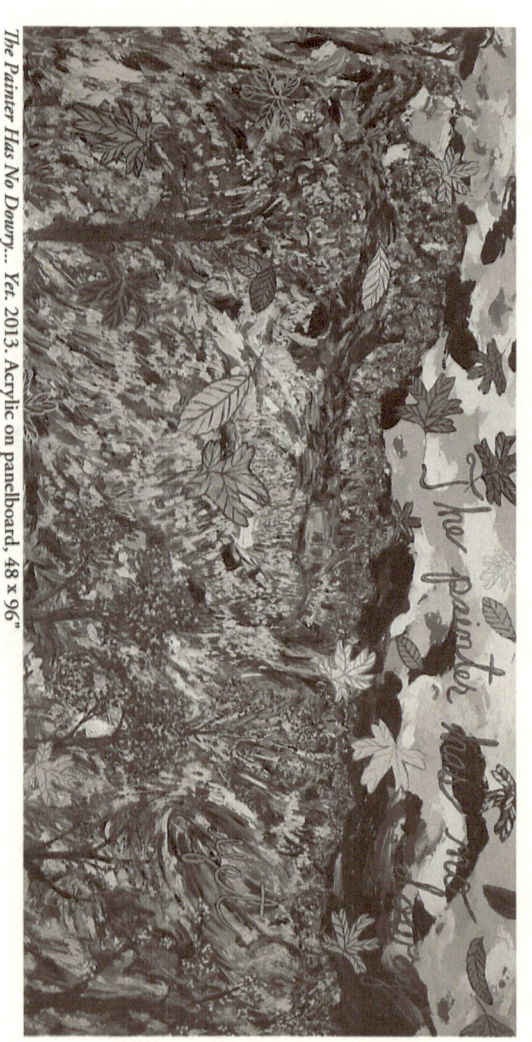

The Painter Has No Dowry... Yet. 2013. Acrylic on panelboard, 48 x 96"

The Painter Has No Dowry

My daughter is getting married and she isn't a reader of this
vitriol. She is not quite a half year out of graduate school, has been
awarded an art teaching position at her high school alma mater,
and is engaged to a good man whom she loves deeply. I think she
stays away from my writing because sometimes it is bile, and she is
one of the strong happy bases in my life who dilutes the acid of me,
and no doubt in the process, often compromises snippets of her
own immediate feelings of well being to do so. Like all daughters
and sons, she is a bit ignorant of the cornucopian hope/worry of
the future her parents imagine for her. The hundred mile commute
to and from her new job in a hundred dollar car. The payback of
student loans at a loan shark interest rate our government sets to
lock up the joy of living to our nation's young and eager. The fear
of return of last autumn's double mononucleosis that found her
worn down from overwork, and paid her dearly for it. We worry
knowing worry is futile. Living check-to-check, from debt-to-debt
is nobodies' joy, yet for the struggling creative artist in America, it can be a season in hell. The work is not an issue. The work
gets done. The paintings amass in piles on the basement floor,
or, if framed, stacked against the wall along the perimeter. You
keep painting and dreaming the painting will pay off, someday.
Brick by brick you build a delusional optimism or succumb to the
madness of failure, which is an internal flame all men share in all
cultures—yet becomes a conflagration to the artist of that culture
who still retains its traditions. I want to be a part of my human
family. But they are embarrassed of me.
    Whether in Tanzania or the U.S.A., all fathers desire a proverbi-
al dowry toward their daughter's wedding day. Here in the states
nuptial traditions are falling by the wayside. The roles are shifting.
Husbands and wives compete for careers. Money flows if you
want money. All can work so the dowry is dead. But the tradition
lingers. Our daughter will make more moolah this month teaching than I have made my whole life as creative writer and painter.
Soon she could support me and pay Rose a dowry to "get Dad off
her back". That is just how the modern global village would have it
be, (no doubt, by virtue of my country's economy stuffing its mon-

ey cheese down the throats of earth's nations). No more traditions. No meals at the table. Both parents off to work at jobs they despise to come home and count the money, which is never enough.

So I fight tradition (as creative painter) yet adhere to it in daily life, maintaining a strict regimen to nuclear family closeness which is a nigh impossible task in a nation replete with personal comfort junkies. Believe me, financially, art does not pay. There lies the painter's frustration, and he may take it out from time to time on curators of museums and galleries. Of course they cannot support him! Their donor's misconceptions of themselves make the artist's delusions look like children's dreams. He wants to be a humble painter. He charges twenty dollars less an hour than a level 9 secretary to the department chair. The garbage man makes fifty dollars more a day than what the artist would want to make in his imagination with strawberries. The dishwasher is on a financial path tenfold more secure than the painter, and the latter gets a social life thrown into the bargain! My city museum claims to support the local artist. I got in a Twitter tiff with a representative the other day. "We've lent our support to 60 local artists in 2012 alone!" He didn't like my essay charging the cult of art with art homicide. "See," he wrote, "We're showing this local guy now." And he links me to a page of an established artist with credentials ranging from write-ups in the New York Times, to gallery hosting of his work in The Museum of Sex. He uses blood to make his art. They're quite beautiful and decorative as far as blood goes. His spotlight is switched on via the several page list of "places where I have tricked art history PhD's into believing I am worthy to invest in". I do not possess that special list which pleases members of the opposite humanity I spam on a weekly basis. I am local, and prefer to be local because I gotta live with these freaking people, I might as well get them to appreciate me, as I do my car mechanic and cashier at the super-duper market. Still, I hope to break through someday to at least one influential member of the elitist crowd who shares my vision of the artist. Just so I can secure a humble dishwasher-income living through my practice. That's it, and that is simple. But it ain't happening, and my daughter's dowry suffers.

For two years I have maintained a "donate" link in the right column of my free blog. Not one penny in charity. I even wrote about offering nickels to the artist as a symbol of support to a vocation that knows no vacation. I have a hundred paintings and several self-published books available for sale, and if it weren't for the kindness of a few good friends and family members, I never would have sold any. It is torture to "make art" in America, where people exchange money every second for a Slim Jim or barbecue potato chip. People here are out of their minds. But in a kind of insanity that is beyond insane (for even the psychiatrists who monitor this behavior cannot see past the noses of their own Slim Jim sensations). Here:

"Most of the young men of talent whom I have met in this country give one the impression of being somewhat demented. Why shouldn't they? They are living amidst spiritual gorillas, living with food and drink maniacs, success mongers, gadget innovators, publicity hounds. God, if I were a young man today, if I were faced with a world such as we have created, I would blow my brains out. Or, perhaps like Socrates, I would walk into the market place and spill my seed on the ground. I would certainly never think to write a book or paint a picture or compose a piece of music. For whom? Who beside a handful of desperate souls can recognize a work of art? What can you do with yourself if your life is dedicated to beauty? Do you want to face the prospect of spending the rest of your life in a straight-jacket?"

—Henry Miller

Well, I am no longer a young man. Then I am either an artist or a supreme fool, for I still believe that I will amass the dowry my daughter deserves. She and my future son-in-law must not pay for their own wedding. If you read this (local friends aside), yet not inquire about the low low price of a Ron Throop painting, then I will go back to line cooking this month or the next. I will be that seedy guy on the broiler who adds a gob of spit to the bubbling butter, just because you were dumb enough to pay thirty dollars for a meal that will last thirty minutes in your mind.

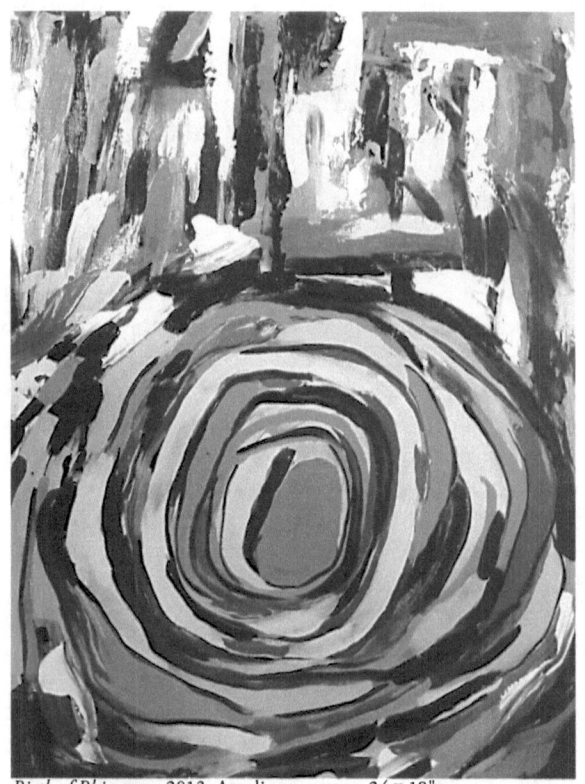

Birth of Rhiannon. 2013. Acrylic on canvas, 24 x 18"

One of the Mood Paintings

The intellectual season almost upon us. I have been working too long without break. I am ready for a fire, a pipe, a stack of books, and high watt artificial light. I want to read a novel out loud to my family while the cold winds blow, and meditate more on the uselessness of despair.

There are too many creative people in all neighborhoods spending their energy on avarice. Most if not all are plagued with the ten thousand things, which provide every distraction besides peace and joy. There is no more time to take time at work or play. People are driving people like cattle, if cattle were also masochists self-saddled with lead weights of illusion. Any one out there know how to get back to basics without going off the deep end?

I am working on a group of abstract paintings that are autobiographical. Whose story do I know better than my own? They're good for contemplation. Unhurried, but not wise. Who will look at them and not think, "Geeze, this guy better get out of the creative business while he can. I could tape ten dipped brushes on my body, go to bed, and wake up with a better product."

Probably true. But what am I to do? Get out of the racket that for me has been no racket? Or, stay true to the fool, and hope this tiny fraction of action has its place in the future of the human race?

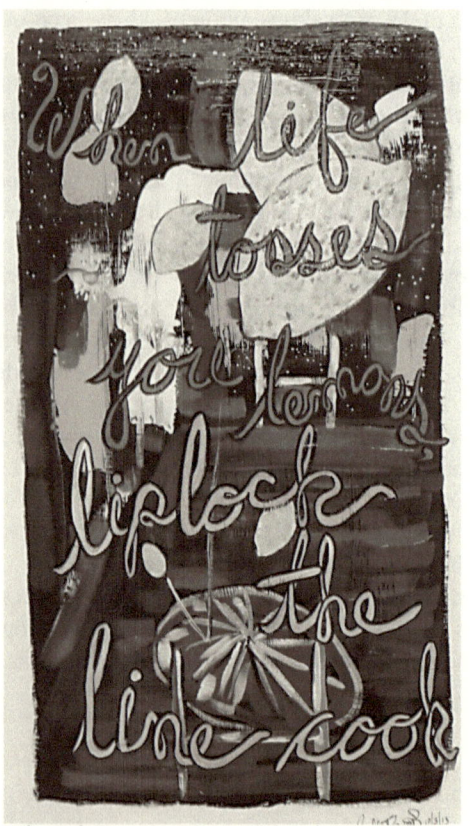

When Life Tosses You Lemons, Liplock the Line Cook.
2013. Acrylic on paper, 22 x 14"

When Life Tosses You Lemons Liplock the Line Cook

Chilly winds. To understand this painting, one must delve into the delusion of a latitudinal synesthete. Clouds and temperature affect my mood, comfort, and creativity like no other natural or man-made phenomena. Nearly twenty years ago during courting of my present day wife and friend, we drove out to the high school football field on a rainy fall night. I had six lemons with me, and a wild urge to throw them deep into the dark. I sent Rose to one end of the field with an umbrella, and from the opposite end zone I launched one lemon after another. She was to mark my best distance. 98 yards at the first bounce.

Earlier that afternoon we picnicked at the park with a bottle of wine and carrot quiche. I had borrowed my friend's car because, although I was poor and happy, I was very weary of the thought that Rose would think she was doomed to walking an entire life time with me. His Trans Am made me feel very sinewy and brave behind the wheel. I knew that Rose knew it was a big fake-out. She understood that I had nothing but my five-year-old daughter.

Wonderful! The night was going perfectly. We set up our picnic under shelter. We drank the wine, ate the quiche, and rushed back to my apartment. What joy the present moment, satisfied in nothing, listening to Dylan's "Mozambique," and "Black Diamond Bay". And with the rain, the rain smells, and the wet, taillight traffic shining out the window, I had to take her back out into the night to do something special for her. Hence the lemons and how seasons and weather play a part in raising the bar of enthusiasm (or is it temporary insanity?) in the determined artist.

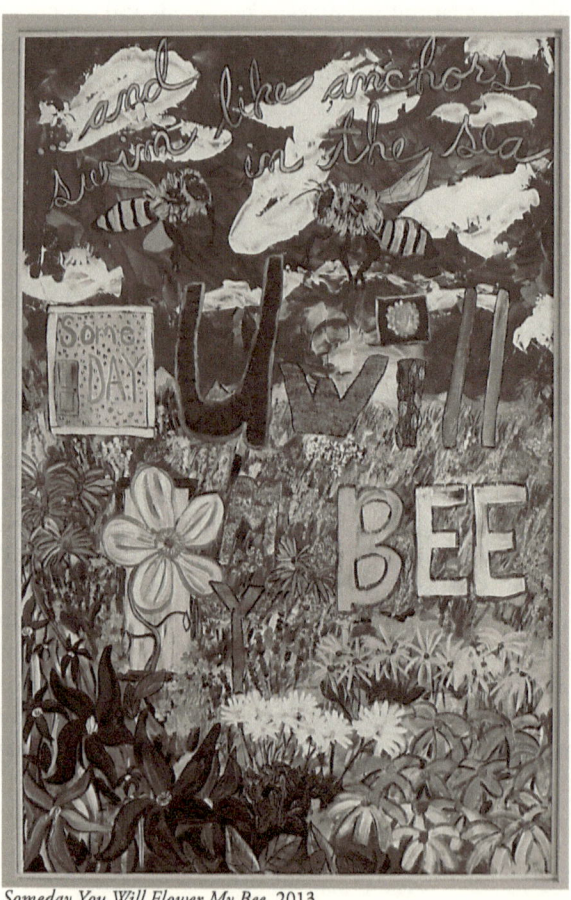

Someday You Will Flower My Bee. 2013.
Acrylic on panelboard, 48 x 32"

David Hockney is Talented and Rich

Went to a painter's site last night and remembered why I should be glad to have been a history major in college. He is a living old man who has six decades of work to view. David Hockney. Never heard of the guy until my cousin, the more knowledgeable painter in the family, referred him to me. I am a man who is rarely interested in the work of others. However, their personal stories thrill me. We all start at the sound shot from the same gun. Some, like David Hockney, end up well known and loved, having strangers from everywhere on earth watch his mid-morning interview live on YouTube.

Others, channeling what appears to be my fate as well, get neither an interview nor a living, no matter how sober (or drunk!), dedicated, and possibly interesting they and their work happen to be. The art market of unartists has no idea how to appraise art until long after all coins have been flipped, landed, and marked on the ledger.

Don't get me wrong. This Hockney is good, having made beautiful paintings that I admire more than anything I have ever done. Color, wow. Form, complete. Skill? Enough to say almost too much. But what is he? What is his story? As a young man inventing style, was he a Wright brother, or more like a Henry Ford? That's where history and biography make their way into the whole art story. It is the birth of creation, the labor pains, growing pains, old age pains that interest me. Never the output, which is arbitrary, subjective, boring really, without the struggle and fire of personality. Hockney painted a chair in the 1970's. So did a multitude of college students at the time. Probably seventy million chairs painted that decade. Was his truly in the top ten? Who says so? History tells me that he got a break. That he was in the right place at the right time. That all artists of good fortune are like colorful pebbles picked from a heavenly (or Hades) stream by a God-child. They have been made at an early age, and by virtue of authentication from these "higher beings" are able to study, hone, magnify their art unto themselves, for self pride and self loathing are the artist's best life weapons.

So I document my story. And if I live to be 76 years old, your children and mine will be able to access on the Internet several decade's worth of Ron Throop work. Poor buggers won't be able to decide for themselves if the paint was worth the mixing. That is the fate of the unknown. The reality of history. Last year some guy bought a house full of art from the sister of a dead local yokel painter. He paid a couple thousand bucks, and the following months had the work appraised by a gaggle of college degrees. A fast three million. And yet the artist willed that they be tossed in a dumpster. Great irony. Super story. A better one than Hockney could ever give to the star makers.

Although no one ever asks me for it, I shall give advice now to fellow artists of the dung heap. Keep at it for posterity. Find strength in the grave silence of galleries and museums. Believe, even if in pretend, that they ignore you because there is only so much time to make money by feeding us some more bland crackers of what has already been digested by the industrial art market. David Hockney maintains two residences in the high end real estate of Los Angeles and its environs. A man who feels would abdicate at least one of these thrones to make room for the life-giving ones. But his sage advice? Keep on drawing.

Bootstraps, bootstraps, bootstraps! He's a Henry Ford for sure.

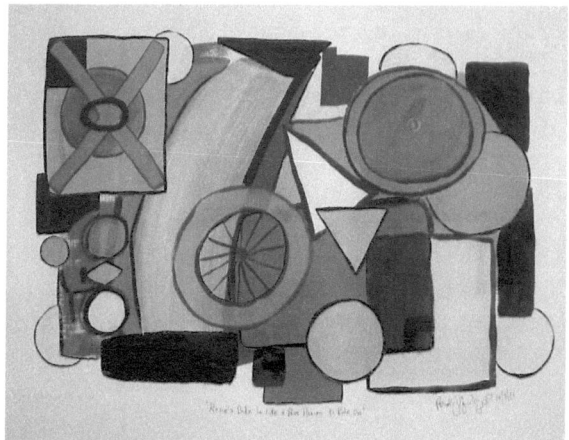

Rosie's Bike is Like a Blue Heaven to Ride On. 2013.
Acrylic on paper, 13 x 21"

So Banksy Made 420 Dollars. Is That a Problem?

That's enough spray paint and stencils for a week, several om-
elets, and a warm coat at the sharing store. I don't see the irony.
I see a very lucky artist. I also see why McDonald's and Walmart
mean so much to us in our gentle insides. We peasants at the altar
of the cult of art praying out the wet dreams of businessmen in
Italian suits. Bishop Banksy has been made. The Pope is any millionaire ready to invest. The common man does not want a black
and white original Banksy except to behave like a millionaire.
Isn't it obvious? The canvases on sale in New York the other day
were worth more than the art that was printed on them. Banksy
knows. I know. What lovers of art and artist need to do now is stop
worshiping false idols, get up off their lazy crumps, make their
own art, or find what their own private wonder loves, and pray to
it. David Geffen is a dirty old man. Art should never have made
this toad richer. Ralph and Ricki Lauren would buy a Banksy to
show their textile slaves how to work harder for less money. We
need to devalue their pieces now. We must de-gentrify the crap

they are over-valuing, especially the historical stuff, which is our crap, humanities' crap. In order to make it Native American like lovers carving initials into oak, we need to congratulate the old dude who made a killing on the street this week. On Sotheby's auction day, a hundred of our most famous must sell their work on the street for a song. Mock every tuxedo they see with a $25.00 original for sale. The bubble will burst only when we stop graduating out of industrial universities more "Hey Spikes!" to tell us what we should like. Christies is hawking porch furniture to gated communities in my art market dreams of the future. Men and women artists are drinking beer along the roadside, playing cards and thinking about dinner.

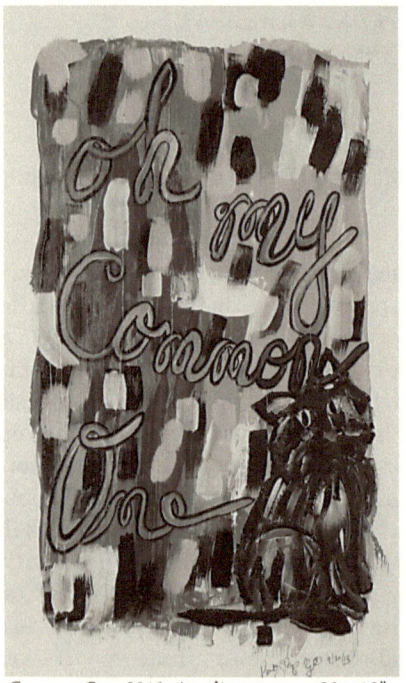

Common One. 2013. Acrylic on paper, 20 x 12"

October 11 Show

I have been deep in basement for past two weeks working on the
joy of man's desiring. The upcoming show in October will be un-
characteristically youthful of me. I am fixing my psyche one baby
newt step at a time. I think it is working, but I won't know for sure
until I have a black disco dress with sparkles, a ballroom to dance
in, and smiling half-strangers who hope for my success in wooing
this beauty beside me.

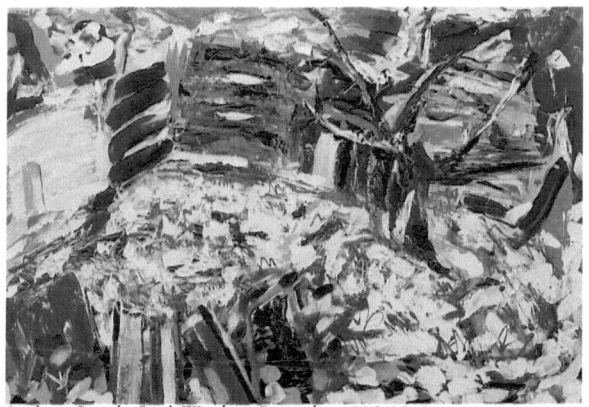

Looking Out the Book Window, December 1995. 2013.
Acrylic on Panelboard, 32 x 48"

Below is part of the introduction to both the literary wonder and
the upcoming invitational in October. The whole house will be
cleared out and the past couple month's of my expressionist love
fire rekindled paintings will be hung on the walls. You can only
come if you're invited because this is a house and a home and there
are just too many riffraffs out and about, not dreaming of art as
much as scamming for free cookies.

This party will cheer. I imagine it to be like the *Time* magazine
spread on the Beatniks back in the 1950's. Jugs of wine passed
around, poetry bouncing off the walls, and a room full of people
getting excited about the upcoming 60's that will bring outdoor
showers and communal tabbouleh. But owing to the present day,
it will probably be somewhat subdued with the exception of *Exile
on Main Street* and Tom Waits' *Bone Machine* shouting from the
speakers. My guests will just have to make do.

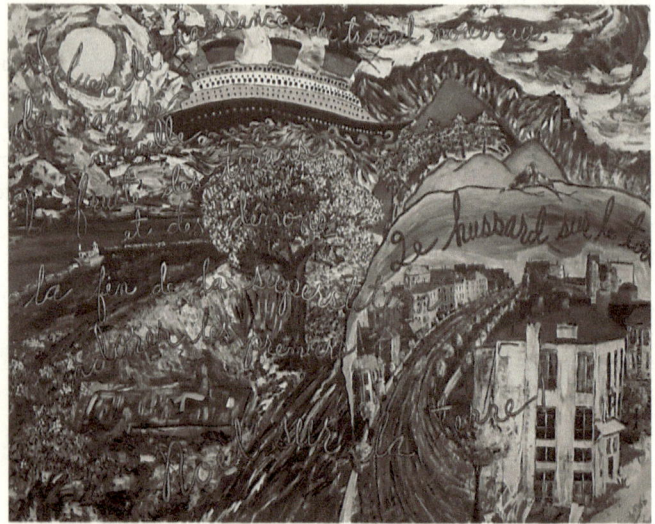

Rimbaud the Line Cook. 2013. Acrylic on panelboard, 48 × 64"

"Thank you for coming. Just showing up is a small mountain moved.

You might be wondering why I chose to open up our house for an art show. Actually it's a one night event, for tomorrow (Oct. 12) I will put the chotskies back on the shelves, and hang the family art and portraits on the walls. I would call this an art party. I organized it for the sake of sanity, and because I ran out of places to show in Oswego. This is wrong for I am a firm believer in clan, that is, local art. And Oswego has never been a good place for the artist to make even the most modest of showings, let alone any kind of minimal minimum wage self-reliance. The town is just too cash poor.

So modern art over the past century and a half has packed up its suitcase and left the village for the big city, where the misfit paint-ers go to be free. There they eat crumbs and drink coffee praying a rich investor on Park Avenue, perhaps a Walton, thinks he needs some poor painter blood to spruce up the front street parlor. Of course he goes to his dealer in Chelsea to tell him which upcoming poor painter will be worth investing in. Otherwise, forget it. Mr.

Walton could pick out a painting for himself like I could partner with an International cargo company to ship my sweatshop textiles and iPhone covers.

Believe me, I get it. Art does not pay. And although I am daft, I am not certifiable. So I married well, yet courted at a time when Rose and I were both poor. (Actually, while she was a student, I was the bread winner. Nine bucks an hour in fact. Big money). At the time I never imagined a future beyond good soup and fresh bread. Why? We had health (still do), a rented roof (still do), borrowed clothes (still do), and National Grid paid on time, sometimes (still do). Today we still live check to check, as do many of us here. I believed then, as I stubbornly do now, that peace and time are the only worthwhile desires, as so much of what makes up a universal good life, can be represented by those two wonderful words. And in a super economy like the United States, even the poor among us, while youthful and strong, can find love, which will carry peace and time throughout an entire life, and also secure a roast chicken on cool autumn nights.

Basically, my life up to this point has been an adherence to this mantra, the only change being that I added a wife and two children into the picture.

I still stubbornly make soup and fresh bread, and paint pictures in a cold room.

Wonderful right? Sure, until that monster hydra, avarice, rears its hideous heads. The dreams of recognition, of actually getting paid to think out loud in color. Ha! Even the painter pretends like Walter Mitty. Who doesn't want to do what he wants to do and get paid for it? It works for some local painters. Those who actually possess rendering talent and can make a landscape look like a landscape that someone would want to look at. For these painters there is always Christmas once a year, and a public that wouldn't mind a Rocky Mountain vista hung above the mantle.

Success for a local expressionist? Let's hope he has enough imagination to power delusion until death, or else pity the poor bugger a prolonged and painful existentialism.

I refuse to sour! My delusion is my non-existentialism.

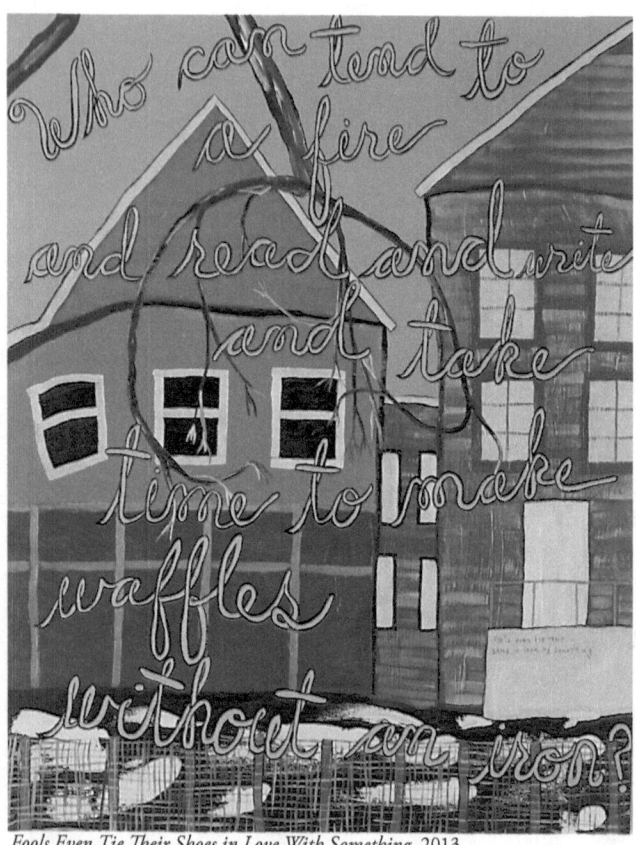

Fools Even Tie Their Shoes in Love With Something. 2013.
Acrylic on canvas, 30 x 20"

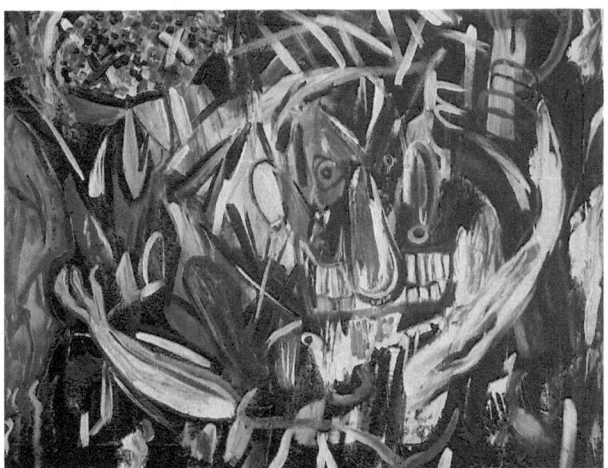

Leaving My Nephew in the Woods to Think About the End of the World.
2013. Acrylic on canvas, 18 x 24"

A Plea to Curators on "Ask a Curator Day"

There are not many worse things to happen to a group of artists
in a community than hearing the news that their mother museum
spent 1.8 million on another dead artist. But they're used to it by
now. The living artists do not need another reminder that their
work is worth peanut shells compared with celebrity dead art. The
Cincinnati Art Museum perpetuates the market for "art we are
told is significant." Ask any painter why he paints, and it is not to
please the mother museum. The latter gave up on the living when
the money-love came to town. She doles out scraps to the living
artist. Makes him competitive among friends in a business that is
anti-business.

Local curators. Please eradicate global think. It is colonialism of
art. The Saatchi Gallery posts photos of Max Ernst on a rocking
horse in 1936 and three thousand people like it after a day. Granted they allow my post, and unlike most international museums,

relegate it to a token space on the page. Still, in his time, Max Ernst was local. Shunned and despised by the majority of curators most likely. Just lucky to be in Paris, at the center of post WWI culture. My God if he was born on a farm outside Tulsa, there's a good chance his hun-hating neighbors would have hung him from a tree before letting him paint what he wanted to paint. Present-day curators are pushing aside artist neighbors in a competitive national-international recognition quest doomed to failure.

Take the Cincinnati Art Museum for instance. Last May I read that they paid 1.8 million dollars to acquire an okay O'Keeffe. It's a 24 x 18 incher entitled *My Back Yard*. Pretty in oil. A dry hill. Sacred like peanut butter and jelly for lunch. As good as any lessor painting gets. She woke up, wiped the sleep out of her eyes, made coffee, evacuated, and then painted a picture.

Mine shown here is the same size as hers but in acrylic. Not only does it have a more provocative title, but there is actual poetry, and perhaps a lesson to be learned. I am asking a reserved bid of $38.00 on eBay—the same price as a fancy iPhone cover, or a full tank of gas.

I believe that any present-day art historian on earth, the self-appointed gatekeeper to public conception of "what is art?" exists solely to poison the living artist. The Cincinnati Art Museum has a million and a half to spend. If it knew art, (which I believe with all sincerity it does not), it would take care of its local artists and use all monies to buy up their work for show after show after show. A hundred supported artists of city and countryside with accepted works that would actually benefit a community. Maybe then an old lady's present day *My Back Yard* would be an oil study of a sunshiny piece depicting her morning at the Cincinnati Zoo. She would get her hundred bucks, and enough boost at self esteem to have herself a go at an Ohio River scene.

Artists do not expect immortal fame. They want to work for pay and pride in whatever locale chosen. The Cincinnati Art Museum is of Cincinnati and has as much moral right to an O'Keeffe as any undeserved billionaire has to it. It did not earn that wealth anymore than the starving artist earns a probable path to self-degradation and spiritual poverty. It mocks the people of its own city and state with an O'Keeffe. Who was this woman? Did she have any connection to Ohio? Nope. Then you can keep it in Santa Fe.

Push it on your own people.

I'll take another approach.

All unknown artists just want to be oboe players in their hometown city symphonies. Paid to do their part. Any oboe dude worth his salt knows that a modest salary awaits if he will just work hard and practice daily. He understands that he will never become a dead Duke Ellington or living Mick Jagger. The city symphony knows too. So they hire him at $20.00/hr. His wife has a job at the college, and they pool their monies each week to pay rent and buy food. Their humble pride fuels a day to day replenishment of enthusiasm. The city symphony supports the oboe artist.

That is city music.

City visual art might have a sidewalk sale, juried show, or fundraising auction to show that it tosses a bone to the local artist every now and then. But unlike the cared-for oboe player, this is no equivalent full or even part-time job support for the sculptor or painter.

Everyone knows what the directors truly pine for—the art equivalent Duke Ellington or Mick Jagger to hang on their walls, to garner reputation (hopefully international), to authenticate their combined PhD's into a giant, institutional glob of security for themselves.

I cannot accept this. I have Syracuse and Rochester to blame. The Everson and Memorial Art gallery directors are ignoring the living artists who stand beside them at local gas stations and super-duper markets. The former are jonesing for their O'Keeffe too. Each has a Picasso piece of toilet paper to show its superior art sophistication to the God host on Mt. Christie's. They toss a bone to lowly locals once in a while. A hundred bucks here, a desktop printed award there...

And then five million for a Duchamp urinal or a Koons balloon.

Local artists of any city I give you the following advice...

Petition your curators to represent you. Invite the community to explore the art of its neighbors. There are traditionalists and dadaists and all expression and mediums in between. Convince the city museum director to sell the 50,000 pencil doodle by Picasso to the Smithsonian or National Galleries, or better yet, some hapless village in Spain where it belongs.

Now to Detroit and the bankruptcy of nations...

You have all heard of the "travesty" in the art world about Christies' appraisal of the Detroit Institute of Arts? For goodness sake, what did they expect? We offer daily prayer to the Christies' host while bored billionaires over value dead art, and likewise add to their own institutional riches, and yet we want to condemn those very auction houses when the phony treasure is taken away. I say sell it all! Get what you can. Let the art museum fail. It's a dinosaur anyway. Something Carnegie-thinking industrialists thought up to reward their broken-backed factory workers. I offer a future that will be both bright and meaningful, and certainly put some pizazz back into art. And if this particular warehouse of art is evacuated, then there are plenty of cheap houses left in the Detroit market to choose from.

Back to Cincinnati where lies a solution to the problem. Its very auspicious existence in the downtown corridor creates the notion of what constitutes art for the community. I have been told over and over again by these self-ordained officiates how local artists are supported by local businesses. Ha! Nothing could be further from the truth. The latter want a photograph of a sunrise or a pastoral painting that is attractive enough and clean. Art that smells like the institution it hangs in. Hospitals and lawyer offices aren't going to hang a urinal in their reception. Neither a Duchamp's nor a Fred Jones' toilet from across the river.

But a museum can and would if curators used their expertise to establish a proud local color. Then visitors to Cincinnati would seek the art its creative citizens have to offer, instead of what some dead influential Parisian thought was cool (and rich industrialist verified with his money) a hundred years ago. Cities across the nation would almost "compete" with their artists; just like professional football in Baltimore would never dig up a dead Johnny Unitas to quarterback. It seeks the fresh flesh... As should curators of galleries and museums. Art is alive. It breathes because the living artist who created it breathes. How much do quarterbacks make when they're dead? Zippy, right? Same with artists. We are human. Any artist out there wanna wait until you're dead to make an honest buck or two? Me neither.

Museums are competing with van Goghs. The people pay their

ticket to see it, are taught by the museum to know what is worthy, some go to college to learn about the worthy and, like Pepsi-cola, that draws its advertisements all over the earth to establish mass bad taste, one day after long and arduous university study, have the position to determine for the rest of us what is art worthy, again and again in perpetuum.

Museums are accountable to their public when they pay over a million bucks for a small canvas well-rendered, but no more or less valuable than any old lady with a careful hand could create. "Ah," says the curator, "but Cincinnati Sally, you didn't know Stieglitz, so here's your fifty bucks lady. Forget about your art. Leave that to us professionals. We know better."

Stieglitz, Stieglitz, Stieglitz! Who cares? The only worthy about him today is if some starving artist dug up his bones and photographed a pastrami sandwich stuck in his jawbone. No wonder most art houses are struggling to exist. They are denying living art. They are throwing a bunch of coffins in Paul Brown Stadium and wondering why attendance is so low.

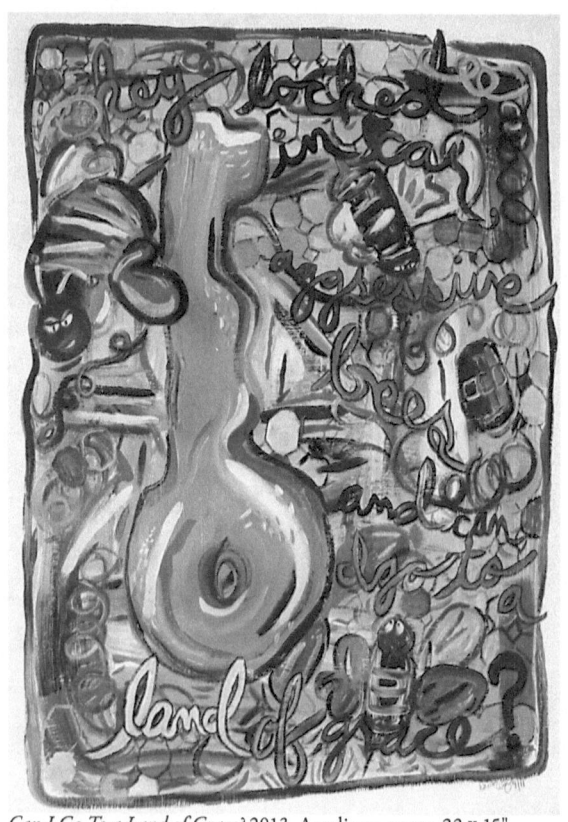

Can I Go To a Land of Grace? 2013. Acrylic on paper, 22 x 15"

The Dalai Lama's Twitter Account

Disclaimer: *Below is my final paper for Coursera social psychology in which I write about my "Day of Compassion", influence my peers, and apply to win a chance to meet the Dalai Lama. Mr. Lama, I am sure, is a kind and gentle human being. I do not wish to offend anyone who follows and applies his teachings. He must deal with slightly depressed, delusional characters like me all the time. Please consider the following essay more tongue-in-cheek clowning around rather than an attempt at thoughtful criticism. Thank you.*

I do not feel much love for the brand *Dalai Lama*. Maybe because twenty years ago, I read through part of a biography about "His Holiness" while my girlfriend sat in the kitchen of our drafty apartment flirting with an old boyfriend who audaciously stopped by on his motorcycle to chat with her. I was "into" spirituality back then, devouring authors who appealed to the hair shirt side of my brain. I read Thich Nhat Hanh—he got me to walk and meditate; histories of Hinduism—they taught me how a poor working father could hold his head high before his daughter; anything by Henry Miller—I was a passionate line cook in America for God's sake, not St. Francis of Assisi. I wanted to woo a mate, and wear my hat like Walt Whitman. I was a romantic and a shy showman, desiring to perfect my life in love with a friend who would help me raise my daughter subsisting on bean soups and warm bread.

I gave up reading the biography to eavesdrop on the kitchen conversation. She wouldn't be "the one", that was for certain. Nor would the Dalai Lama. Too much money, not magic, in the making of his brand. I wanted men who suffered first and then found enlightenment, not coddled children who got hand-picked by golden-robed men to be religious kings. The Buddha left his wife and child to find enlightenment? My God, what a coward! I was a twenty-five year old American flopdoodle, yet even I knew better. Siddhartha ran away from true responsibility. Went and sat under a tree, leaving his kid back at the palace to wonder for the rest of his life why daddy left home. And that suffering wheel the Buddhists chant about while bowing along humble walks to oblivion... Obviously the boy grew up and abandoned his own children, either figuratively or literally.

Buddha rose above the wheel of life and death, and left his family to suffer karma.

What a selfish narcissist!

"They like to take all this money from sin/
  build big universities to study in,
  Sing Amazing Grace
  all the way to the Swiss banks"

—Bob Dylan

So this day of compassion I have led... What of it? What came to be? Did it change our President's mind about bombing helpless children in Syria? Did it prevent the Dalai Lama from stepping into another jet airplane to whisk his wisdom around the globe, while stuffing a dirty sock down the throat of our atmosphere? Did it make me stop and be mindful of the man I dream to be? No more or less than any other day since I have decided to not take the path, but become it. Yes, perhaps I am delusional to the point of actually teaching the Dalai Lama a thing or two about "right living", the Eight-fold Path, that yarn about "Have you had your supper? Then clean out your bowl Bingo!"

I read in my 2009 edition of the Myers' book about the "sadder-but-wiser effect" demonstrated by mildly depressed people. I quote at length to shed light of how susceptible professionals are to avarice, the powerful vice preventing our living Rimbaud's "Christmas on earth":

Normal people exaggerate how competent and well-liked they are. Depressed people do not. Normal people remember their past behavior with a rosy glow. Depressed people are more evenhanded in recalling their successes and failures. Normal people describe themselves primarily positively. Depressed people describe both their positive and negative qualities. Normal people take credit for successful outcomes and tend to deny responsibility for failure. Depressed people accept responsibility for both success and failure. Normal people exaggerate the control they have over what goes on around them. Depressed people are less vulnerable to the illusion

of control. Normal people believe to an unrealistic degree that the
future holds a bounty of good things and few bad things. Depressed
people are more realistic in their perceptions of the future. In fact,
on virtually every point on which normal people show enhanced
self-regard, illusions of control, and unrealistic visions of the future,
depressed people fail to show the same biases. "Sadder but wiser"
does indeed appear to apply to depression. Taylor, S.E. (1989) Positive Illusions: Creative self-deception and the healthy mind. New
York: Basic Books. (p. 516)

Looks like all the "normal" people are getting their daily soma
pill, while the wise ones are prescribed anti-depressants to "dress
up" their bummer reality.

My mother has a mantra, not likely to be repeated on rice beg-
ging walks throughout Lhasa. I tend to agree with it more than
any empty philosophy uttered by a holy man from a Palo Alto
hotel room.

It is this:

Charity begins at home

I have deep compassion for my immediate family, my wife and
children, my ingroup. Yet it is never enough. Yes, I am prejudiced
to all outgroups, no matter how large or small. No, I do not feel the
need to feed the poor, clothe the homeless, instruct the ignorant.
I want to teach myself and those whom I can truly influence, the
joy of life. That is the true wheel. Wisdom shared from parents to
children. I believe that being mindful of our responsibility to the
next generation, that is, to raise children with the utmost care and
kindness, is the only worthwhile profession.

And then avarice rears its ugly head. The economy improves year
after year. The money is there, also the mortgage, the two cars, the
cable, the supermarket, the retirement, the "me, me, me" pumped
up on methamphetamine. Children potty-trained then day-cared
to professional babysitters. Our own professions calling us to
depart in mind, body and soul for the majority of our awake time.
Childhood depression, stress on the freeway, and Freddy grows up
wanting to become a Zen Buddhist. The wheel of suffering turning
and turning, my own professor assigning a "day of compassion",

personal Bodhi trees for all the parents out there agonizing over a Lexus car payment.

I wrote the following in a letter to my daughter for her high school graduation. I include it to shed light on the generation (let alone cultural) gap:

"In an interview Noam Chomsky once admitted that he did not expect, nor even encourage his children to share a similar world view. I don't think that is possible considering his fame and misfortune as a world renown humanist. Perhaps by stating publicly their ignorance of his politics, he would prevent future Army Ranger raids on the cribs of his grandchildren. Either way it is wrong thinking. Here is a man alive today who wants to drastically change the public's perception of the American Empire, yet leave his children 'off the hook'.

Geez, if he can't persuade his own flesh and blood at the dinner table, then how is he going to achieve moral revolution to the millions of minds of a sick society? Doomed to failure, don't you think, if his own spawn cannot be convinced?

Well, I am no Noam. Sure I have opinions, but most are formed in the gut. My gut persuades me to believe that it is a more reliable reader of our political world than the eyes, ears, and encyclopedic inner wanderings of Noam Chomsky's well documented gray matter.

Surely there is something to be said about his ignoring the kids. Is Noam any different kind of careerist than the bank vice president? I mean it takes a lot of time out of a person's day whether he is an astute member of the board or a genius in sneakers. Loans to sign, books to read, lunch to eat, books to write, desk arrangement, office hours, thousand dollar plate fundraisers, speech invitationals, an immoral philosophy to uphold, a moral philosophy to uphold... So much in common when there is not a minute of free time to teach the children. Really, why have kids if there is no intention to pass on a philosophy?"

My question to be answered by the Dalai Lama if ever I meet him on a Stanford sidewalk is this:

What's up with your Twitter account? 7,636,789 followers, but you follow no one? Is that the path to enlightenment? Compassionate arrogance? I would think that a spiritual leader who wants to connect with as many people as possible, to be ever mindful of their love and hope and dreams, would at least follow the many who follow him. You want us all to be in touch? Then you must be in touch. Open the flood gates and leap into the suffering tsunami of humanity. Or become the true path, the raccoon, the camel, the hummingbird, who have known all along, that there is no enlightenment outside of teaching your young. Ah, but when that is done to the best of our human abilities, like it was without the help of antibiotics fifteen thousand years ago, the same Heaven and Hell will be known again to all living things.

Until that day returns, it's all topsy-turvy in the human world.

So, at first light on the morning following my day of compassion, I will bake some baguettes and sift through the cat litter. Exactly what I have been doing almost every day for the past fifteen years.

Maybe in the next life I'll be picked up for future international fame from some Himalayan village off the beaten path. Perhaps not. More likely I'll be a shy goat chewing tin cans while his holiness is placed onto the royal Lhasa litter. But that is neither here nor there. Thank you for this chance, Professor P. and staff, to clean up my mind the last several weeks. I really enjoyed your class.

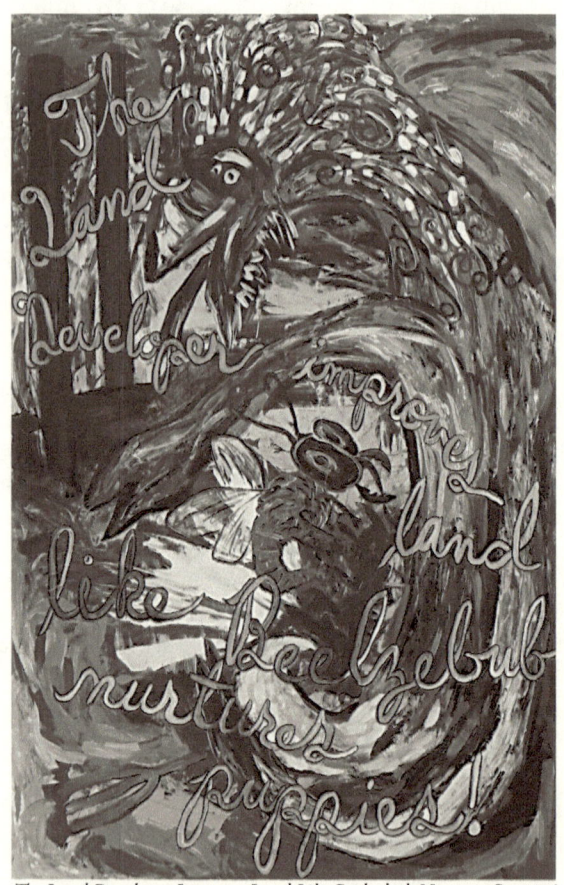

The Land Developer Improves Land Like Beelzebub Nurtures Puppies!
2012. Acrylic on panelboard, 48 x 32"

Throop Resume

Although I have been painting regularly for over twenty years, I did not come out of the cellar to show until October 2008, when I turned 41. Hence the shortlist. All in New York, except France.

2013 Two MoMAtalks' posts:
http://momatalks.tumblr.com/post/55433470901
http://momatalks.tumblr.com/post/60286381255
2013 To be published in 2014 volume of *Stone Canoe*, an art journal
10/2013 Group show 4th Friday at Artist's palette, Norwich.
10/2013 Solo show *Leopold Courting Rose,* Our House, Oswego.
10/2013 Group show invitational *Achromatic* at AAO, Oswego.
7/2013 Solo show *Paper Paintings* at Farden Gallery, Sterling.
7/2013 Group show *Fracking Flow* at Smithy Arts Center, Cooperstown.
3/2013 Best in Show at Lakeside-Statewide at AAO, Oswego.
2/2013 Performance Art, 601 Tully, Syracuse.
12/2012 Member's Show, Rochester Contemporary, Rochester.
10/2012 8-day Residency in Montcabrier, France.
10/2012 Solo show *End of the Line* at AAO, Oswego.
9/2012 Art on the Lawn at Cooperstown Art Association, Cooperstown.
7/2012 Honorable mention at Member's Show at AAO, Oswego.
5/2012 Juror's Citation in *Essential Art* at CAA, Cooperstown.
5/2012 Group Show "Text As Art", Troy.
3/2012 Admission into Schweinfurth Museum, Auburn.
7/2011 2nd place in Member's Show at AAO, Oswego.
5/2011 Solo show *Why Paint Words* at AAO, Oswego.
3/2010 Best of Show at Lakeside Statewide at AAO, Oswego.
7/2010 2nd place in *Member's Show* at AAO, Oswego.
7/2009 1st place in Member's Show at AAO, Oswego.
2/2009 Solo show *Either Books or Children* at SUNY, Oswego.
3/2009 Honorable Mention at Lakeside Statewide at AAO, Oswego.
10/2008 Solo show *Either Books or Children* at Zollo's, Oswego.
3/2008 Honorable Mention at Lakeside Statewide juried event at AAO.

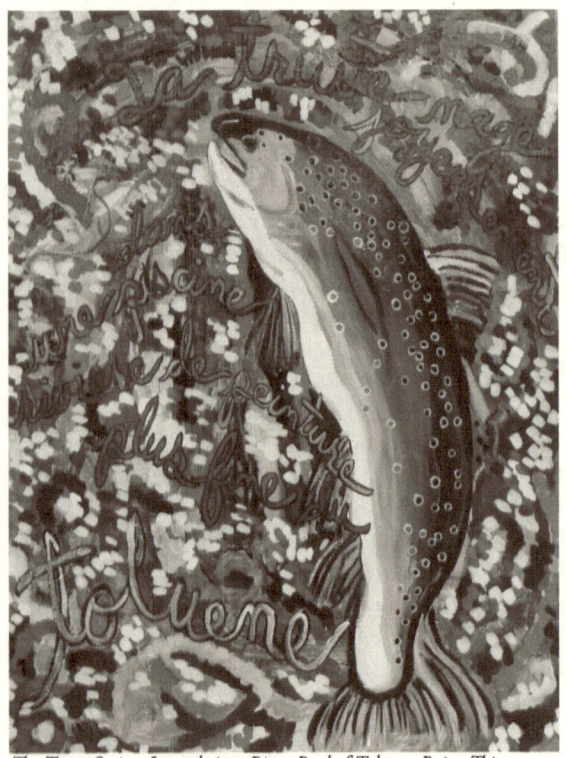

The Trout Swims Joyously in a River Pool of Toluene Paint Thinner.
2012. Acrylic on hardboard, 18 x 14"

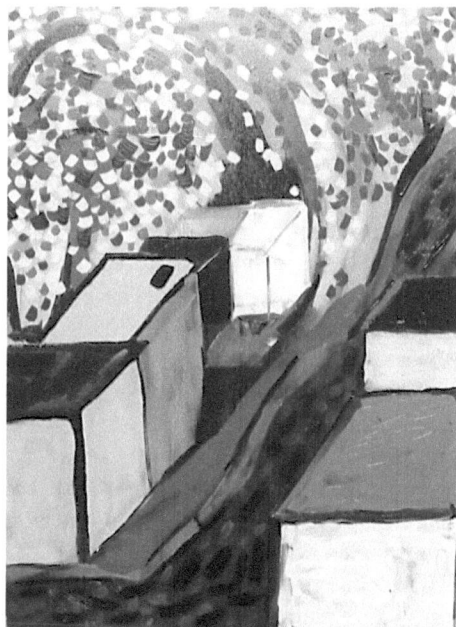

Poverty Street. 2013. Acrylic on canvas, 24 x 18"

Grant Application

Lately I have felt the strong desire to get up on a soap box (where can I get one?) and Niagara Falls all my failure frustration to other non-paid artists and writers inhabiting this ADHD economy Disney-wasteland. What, pray tell, are we going to do?

Well, this shy painter is nonplussed no more. I know the enemy. To take to the public road in order to confront him, either to parley or to smite, is to be like an attractive Cheyenne girl, lost on the Chisholm Trail, asking for directions at a midnight cowboy bachelor party—doomed to failure big time.

No longer surprised at the conspiracy of silence, I realize now that all the post-grads have ever known about the process of art, is how to get a job in the stream of it. Consummate overseers to the wealthy ranchero class, they are well-received, drunken Ricks and Roys, having a go at the poor lost girl. Sure they'll give her directions. After raping her spirit.

Below is my letter to the Pollock-Krasner Foundation. They refused me this spring. And I refuse to parley with their smartphone overseers, (like if I ever get the chance!). They are simply too rude. Jackson Pollock would have let me ride his bicycle, and made a gift of big canvas and paint. I would have handed him the rights to the finished work, as long as he cut me a check for groceries or the electric bill. We, no doubt, would have understood each other on a professional level.

Picasso: "When art critics get together they talk about form and structure and meaning. When artists get together they talk about where you can buy cheap turpentine."

New York critics don't get art. Polite whiners may only dream of the poor Indian girl. After the public party these movers and shakers return to $2500/month rental units to watch cable TV. Ring...ring. "Did you hear that Lady Ga-gag turned off her Twitter account? Yeah, the poor poet-painter finally shamed that awful clown of a human being into creating a conscience. Is she still going Gagosian? Hope so. I need material for the column."

Save it for the N.Y. Times. It is no stranger to spamming artistss who can barely get 20 bucks a painting.

Art is alive and well.
Just not in New York.

Now for the grantor class:

Dear members of the grant committee,

I am applying for the Pollock-Krasner Foundation Grant because I am a determined man. Unlike Henry Miller who arrived in Paris at the age of forty suspecting that he was an artist but needing six months of stimulation-by-poverty to prove it, I have known all my life that I am another one in a long line, both ignored and distinguished, to have the (mis)fortune of that mysterious element "X" inside me. I am forty-six years old, home teaching a twelve-year-old daughter, and retiring every night into a basement studio with my music and paints.

This has been my practice for over twenty years. I have taught our other daughter (age 23) until high school, working as a line cook to make ends meet, and an artist at every free moment to tame the element "X". I have written and self-published six books with provocative titles and very few readers, had several self-sponsored shows exhibiting my work, and putting our family in deeper debt year after year. One could say that to the present day, my life has painted its own tribute to a persisting in folly that might make a Jackson Pollock envy another fool.

Professionally I have remained an enthusiastic failure. That is I buy paints, canvas, wood, frames, work feverishly, and have over the past five years, joined the unsaid "show circuit", exhibiting my paintings wherever and whenever possible, always at my own (and wife Rose's) expense, having few if any sales in Oswego, N.Y., and yet getting up after falling down again, and again, and again.

And now to the glee of our credit card company, I have discovered big and expressive.

For my friend's birthday this week I delivered to his hovel, *She Got on a Train in Taos*. It's a five-foot piece in acrylic about his new love affair before the great sleep. He's in his fifties, an artist optimist, berry picker, a deeply sensitive and good man who, by virtue of social networking, convinced a woman he knew in high school (a fabric artist living in Taos) to drop everything gained to spend life (frigid winters) with him in Oswego, N.Y. They are *pobre pero sana* (poor, but healthy) making colorful dresses and fabric art out of recycled materials. I'll include the painting in one of my ten images. They were so happy to get an authentic proof of their commitment that they have foregone official marriage for the time being, and will look to the painting as a wedding band.

For years I have painted relatively small and compact, as funds would allow. There's a college next door that sells smooth Bristol paper for two dollars per 30 x 40" sheet and Golden paints for enormous sums. A 2 ounce tube for twelve dollars goes far enough for miserly painters, and I have been very careful to stretch the paints out smooth for economy. However this year I have discovered big. The painting mentioned above is comically rendered, not at all where I want to go with paint.

I foresee brave, broad stokes with wide brushes across eight foot canvas, and palette knives replaced with old record album covers. I have always worked fast, but now desire more of an unhurried dance to my painting. Forever confident in application of color and contrast, I now feel the pressing need to let go like the sage. When I day dream this possibility I feel a tingling in my fingertips. That is joy and optimism! It is what I seek for my future as a painter.

And then the realty of living check-by-check becomes all too real, and I find myself fermenting country wines to supplement income to justify expensive paints. I shop at A.C. Moore holding my 40% off coupon to buy inferior pigment that dries as drab as a February day in Oswego. I am seeking your foundation's help to free me as an artist, to open up the door of giving myself, expressively, routinely, until it is my turn for the great sleep.

Practically that means an upgrade to bulk gallon jars of paint and much larger surfaces. I could still work out of my basement but would need help to secure storage. Ideally I would rent a studio, but I don't know if this kind of funding is available through the foundation. As usual I would finance my own yearly show in hopes of acquiring sales, a probability much improved with the auspices of a Pollock-Krasner grant.

Thank you for the opportunity to apply. All determined artists must find themselves in great financial need from time to time. Whatever their success in obtaining funds, nothing compares to a morale boost from an established artist, present or past. The foundation would improve my chances at success tenfold with barely a head nod and a five dollar cash prize. Pollock and Krasner had suffered enough in struggle to gain respect and self-assurance in their artistic endeavors. They are the people who, if living, would invite a kindred spirit and his wife to dinner. I already receive their blessing from the clouds. I could really use the foundation to authenticate it on paper.

Best wishes,

Ron Throop

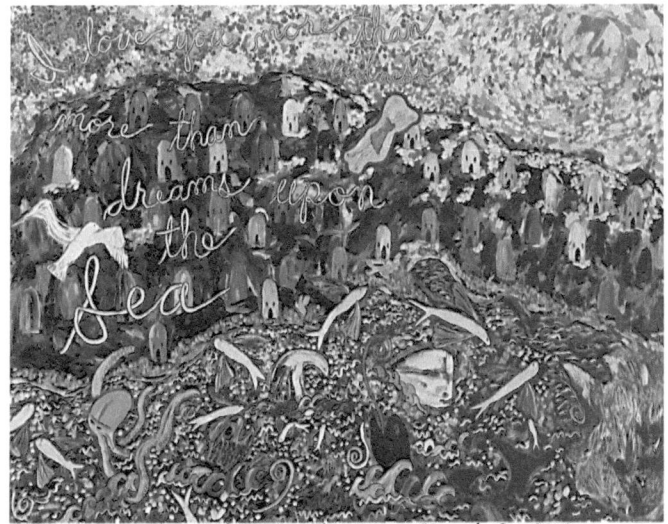

I Love You More Than Madness More Than Dreams Upon the Sea. 2013.
Acrylic on panelboard, 48 x 64"

Answering "What Makes Art" for Agora Art Gallery

Art is and always will be the artist. Henry Miller taught me that.
Over many books time, and he never let up. Miller's efforts and the
luck of my birth into a super-economy, cleared a path for fools like
me to take a chance to be grown-up and an artist in ways that he
never could. That is, I could tap from my high kinetic potential,
(which is top on list of prerequisites for art and artist), to raise a
family creatively and yet still be true to myself.

We do not get rich, and yet unlike the actual imposters to art
(Christie's, the Town of Chicago, and Jeff Koons) we need not seek
continuing education classes in prostitution. Miller was immune
to outside authentication. It helped that he got a masterpiece published that made the yacht Long Islanders and Hollywood fiends
tolerate a clown-nihilist. For the dumbed-down of his age, *Cancer*
loosened inhibition for spousal exchange and basement pornog-
raphy, which happens to be the norm on high definition cartoon
television today. And group think never recognized his high con-
tribution to the life worth living after the "dirty books". Likewise,

in my late middle age, I have yet to meet anyone who "gets" Miller like I do.

So he would go to Monterey and hawk his watercolors on the street. I take my paintings to the woods to chastise the bee and the bear.

Read *Stand Still Like the Hummingbird*. Read *Big Sur and the Oranges of Hieronymus Bosch*. The reason they exist is because of Paris, 1932 and an oceanic leap of faith that only and ever an artist (and art) can take. Americans would want him to dig a ditch, the bum. Drop dead of a heart attack. Listen on the radio to how the new Ivy League President Roosevelt will safely shape the peasant's future and save him from the likes of Dutch Schulz and Al Capone. Nothing has changed. Henry Miller wins. I win.

The art world is still zero.

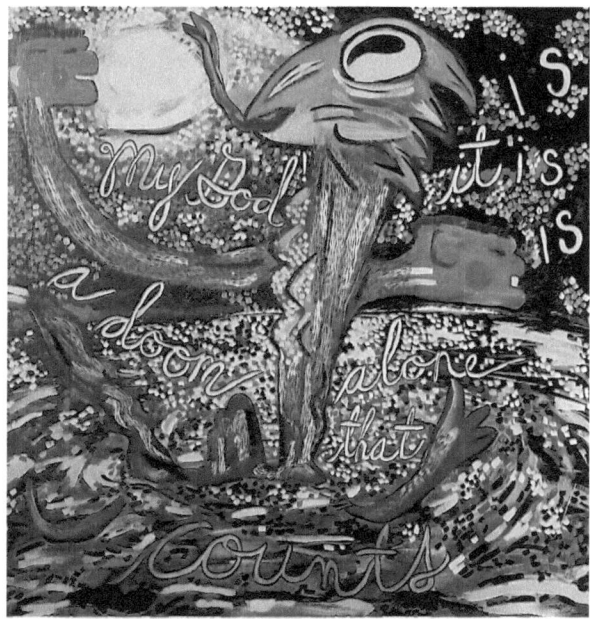

It Is Is Is A Doom Alone That Counts. 2013.
Acrylic on canvas, 36 x 36"

What is the Value of Art?

For this painting? Exactly $188.43. Why? Because I spent 10 hours of my life working on it. And my wife suggests that I charge at least a $10/hour wage. For the canvas (1½" thick generic), I used a 40% off coupon at an A.C. Moore 30 miles away. With gas money and Golden Acrylics added in, plus sales tax, I get to the above figure, which is exact.

That is its monetary value.

Its intangible worth is another story. A long one. A novel in twelve volumes; the fourth where I finally divulge my true intentions with the piece above. I began the morning in a funk, feeling sorry for the painter alive in a nation that boasts an impossible super economy, yet trounces its good fortune with an F350 sensitivity to life. Squash the spider! Swat the fly! Watch an eight year old smash a thousand exoskeletons fleeing up the anthill to protect it.

I spent the early morning spam tweeting a hundred gallerists to make them wake up to the prolific potential I have always hyper-activated in hard copy for my village. Then a wake-up call to my twelve year old daughter whom I homeschool away from the F350's—to teach her that diesel is death, yet antibiotics has opened the door to the greatest party that will ever be. We need to live creatively (and quietly) alongside the diesels, so that we can dream *Christmas on earth* without interruption.

This thinking cheers me to an idea that ferments throughout the morning and into late afternoon. I prepare a scratch meal while waiting for my wife to come home from work. She arrives, plops down in the chair and we unload our thoughts for the day.

Dinner and more talk. A trip to the country wine cellar and a blank canvas in the basement.

Go!

I used to rock back and forth in my bed as a boy. I would set three albums on the turntable and let them play through while I rocked myself to sleep. Every single night of my life from age 11 to 18, when college roommates were enough peer pressure to make it a private affair with the door locked.

Now in my basement studio some twenty odd years later, I have gone back to rocking out all of that dreamy energy from my arms and eyes via painting. This night I was going to give my wife a hard copy that would sell. A nature scene at night of our Great Lake Ontario. No more politics. No more cultural critic. Finally a landscape some home decorator would purchase for $188.43. And it started out that way, innocent enough, probably Van Morrison singing "Oh my love when I am away from you..." And all the proposal promises I tacitly made with my lover were kept. We saved for our children's college. We went to a camp in the summer and cuddled up on the couch to watch TV on stormy nights.

I might have kept to Van for an hour replaying, *Summertime in England*, and got bold with my love in a red dress, painting soft strokes while slow dancing with her in pacific moonlight. Then suddenly *Harvest Moon*, and I discover the demon rumors are true. He is rising from the lake! The creature writhes inside every single one of us. No escape. Both rickshaws and diesel trucks. All are accounted for in mortality. Holy Jesus, we're gonna die!

So the following night I let the born again nihilist Bob Dylan set my text to the painting. It reminds us that doom is impossible to avoid at the onset of middle age.

Even with remarkable advances in metallurgy and sleek rubber linings, the shiny new Ford 350 will rust and leak by the time we are fifty.

It is (is is) a doom alone that counts, and that is the value of art to the living.

This particular piece should remind its buyer that there is no doubt, in a super economy, only a hardened, bitter, and frightened man will buy something he can afford.

So, any takers? I'll have to add $45.00 for shipping.

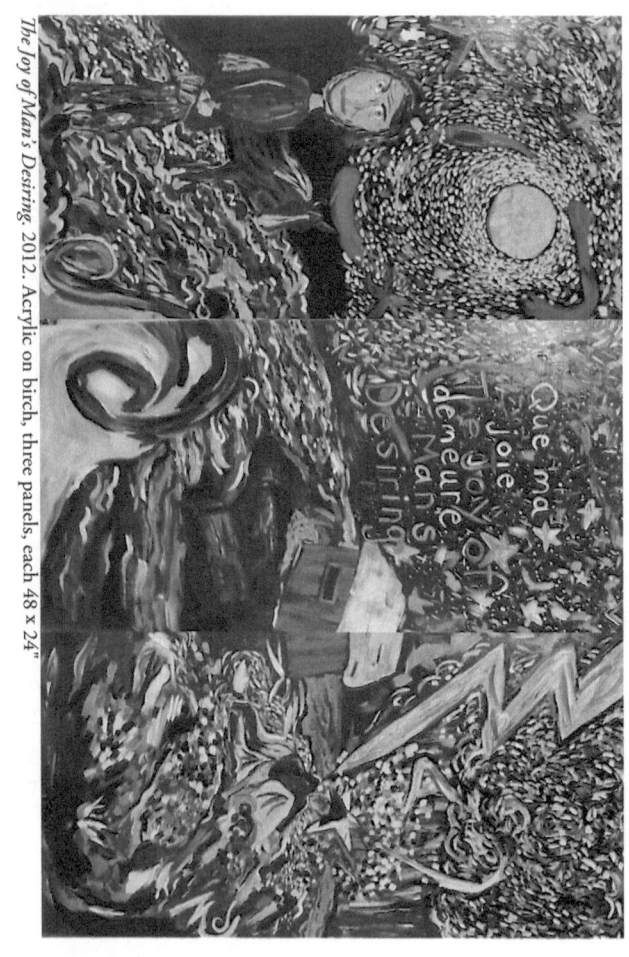

The Joy of Man's Desiring. 2012. Acrylic on birch, three panels, each 48 x 24"

Answer to Agora Gallery's Twitter Question "Is Art Urgent?"

When viewing the work of an artist I seek the biography of the man/woman expressed in hard copies. I mark the energy of the joy or angst living in each piece. If there isn't any, there isn't art. Easy marker. With that said, allow me to cite a piece of yesterday that I hope will help answer this important question.

Early in the day I shared with my wife a break time video of Tom Jones and Janis Joplin back in 1969 singing and dancing "Raise your hand". I wrote to her that this is what gurgles through my veins most days.

Go watch it on YouTube (skip corporate commercial): www.youtube.com/watch?v=jXlP7PyaHdA

Did you see it? Got up and danced, yes? Made you almost feel ashamed to live in a land that has warped the meaning of joy and dance (which is often art) into Beyoncé, a phony by-product of Proctor and Gamble, Coca Cola, or AT&T smartphone toothpaste glued to your face:

www.youtube.com/watch?v=OdeyqChOSwk (2013 Super Bowl).

Not ever, even in a very weak moment, say solitary confinement in a boy's prison or island castaway, would I be interested in the choreographed faux-dance of Beyoncé. It is without real desire. I think it hasn't loved since it was a little girl. It says "Me" like a midnight moon, never a blazing sun. All in all, I think Beyoncé hates art, and has sent her husband into gallery show rooms to rap about it.

Her dance is not an "outward expression of an inward harmony of the soul." It is, to me, a kind of death of individuality and its right to expression. Poor Beyoncé. She is just a tool, as were Tom and Janis in their day to a degree. The difference is in their humanity. That unlikely 60's couple each got to dance like any nerd in the lunch line and feel good about it. Real good. Today the corporations steer us to do the impossible and copy the world's champions, which sets up stone walls to our dance as expressive creatures. Then this negativity gets revealed in our every day lives: Paint a picture? Not if you can't out dance both van Gogh in color and Wyeth in boredom. Chisel marble? Are your balls square? There has been only one superstar worthy of that! The world's champions, (a Kurt Vonnegut idea), existed in 1969 too. Yet from watching the "Raise Your Hand" video (I was 2 years old at the time thinking about becoming a painter), it is so obvious to me that the door was open for humanity (at least for those existing in a healthy economy) to virtually explode with creativity per capita.

Art's urgent task is to reopen that door. It must go back a generation to Tom and Janis, further back to the Mohawk and Santee Sioux; I say shine light on the first clan even, to notice how Glub the Firestarter turned a rock into a Mastodon with his smoldering magic stick. Hurrah! Let's party!

And Glub's brothers and sisters gesticulate the wild human dance while drinking spit beer late into the night.

Beyoncé, Jeff Koons and Rita the corporate-sponsored conceptual artist who uses her feet to throw rocks at spider monkeys, are invaders in our once deeply expressive village. ABC and PBS are working overtime this week getting us to authenticate their celebrity. This will sell more Crest, more Toyota Corollas, and less and less of the truth that each and every one of us is deeply expressive if we dare to dig that deep. The entertainers can be amazing and excite us to our own expressive joys, which is art manifest. I got up and raised my hand with Tom Jones, but I didn't want to be like him. I writhed and wrinkled and spilled my spit fermented beer on the hide carpet. I woke up and painted a saber-toothed tiger stalking a Super Bowl celebrity into the forest.

Art must coax art out of the box that money and power have stuffed it into. Museum is art history. Instrumental in preserving art's stories. However, no joy comes from paced, clockwise observation at a respectable five foot distance, whether that be an afternoon at the Louvre or your local, struggling art association. And celebrity is anything but celebratory. Lady Gaga is Cindy Sherman. Mick Jagger is Jasper Johns. Millionaire super jocks with dead style choreographed. I think their art is as much fun to be around as burning plastic. It is urgent that we support the expression of our neighbors Donna, who paints us the real news, (what the fourth estate has abandoned for advertising deals), and Fred, the marble sculptor sweating out angst in the oppressive July heat. His suburban neighbors doze the live long day in the cool of the swimming pool.

Hey, crank up the music. *Yawn.* Just another Beyoncé tune.

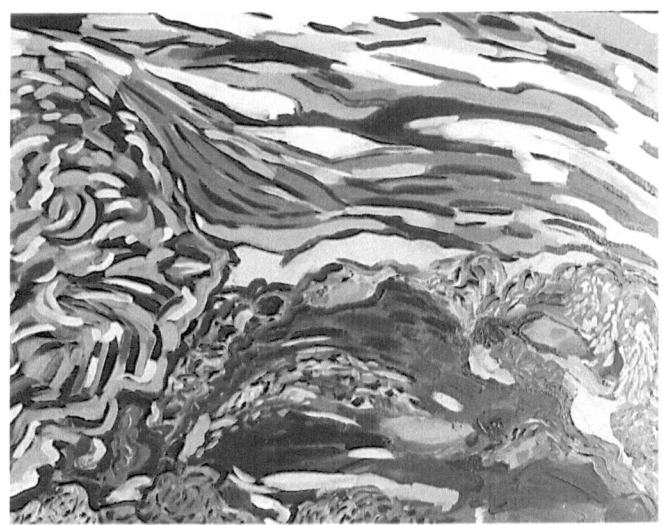

Walking Home With Scott and Matt in 1980. 2013.
Acrylic on canvas, 18 x 24"

Yesterday's Typing Fragmentals With Friends

Just in case I am feeling expressive today, I brought along
this 1950s typewriter, a relic of love, to teach me a thing or
two about verve on a Sunday.

I am famous in Cooperstown.

Dan suggests a mystery. For him the scene of the crime will
never be on eBay, not even if all evidence points to that URL.
Dyed Stitches is set up in the parking lot. A couple more
hours of this and my ear hair will grow out an inch.
I am sorry Dan, but I cannot hear you.
Typing in my ear hair.

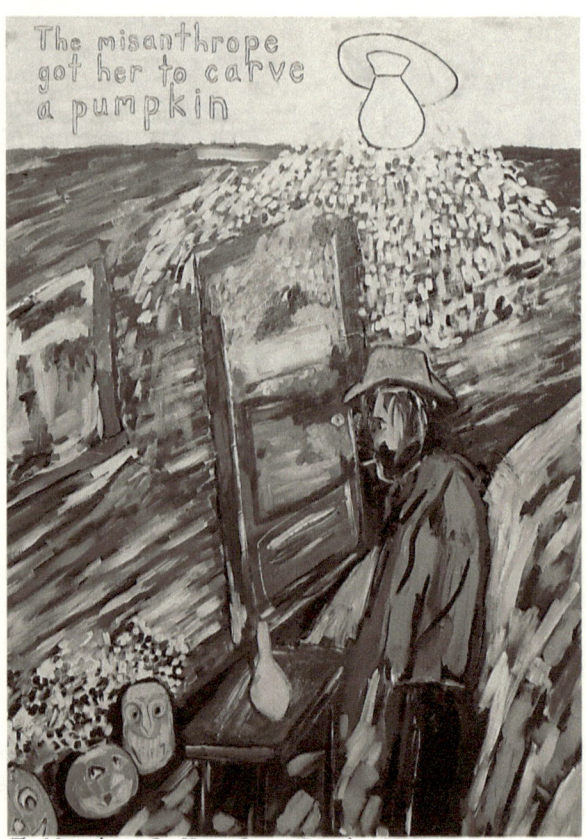

The Misanthrope Got Her to Carve a Pumpkin. 2013.
Acrylic on canvas, 30 x 20"

All I keep seeing with this parade of humanity are bare
toes and the wonder when anyone last paid attention to in the
shower.

Customers,
Go away. I hate business.
"How much do you want for that I'm going to the store.
Man says 'three dollars',
All right, I'll give you four."

— Bob Dylan Poor Boy

More toes
My eyes can smell them.

Jill is a writer. She took typing in the seventies', and her
penmanship is neat. If my writing was judged by neatness,
I'd be a handless speed monkey leaping on love letters with
foot smears.

I have a permanent itch I cannot scratch.
Bipedalism.

Adult sunglasses? Gross.

Smoking in a wheelchair? Authentic cynicism.

Arms are funny for an appendage.
They look fishy. No, froggy.

There's a psychic to my right
psychos to my left.

I like selling with Dan and Jill.
I think I have a "trusting" look.
Good balance to their shady characters.

Dan is away doing the "Dead Walk Manning".
Are there many lesbian couple vendors at Further

concerts?
  Rose thinks so.
  Her and Jill are partners.

I think she photographs me because I am a laughing hyena
without tricks.

Rose, keep your chest off their eyes!
Dan is back.
He met a girl.

I will have someone to buy a boat for me. A butler for
purchase, delivery, captaining,
  the works.
  Rose and our friends will float in the shade with cold drinks
and
  fruit.
  Then we wake up in realland and count eachother's sleep
creases.

A Bovine sad song:

"If you don't know me by now
You will never-ever know me as a cow."

I feel like kickin' Cosmic Charlie the Can Man in the hump-
back. Damn poser!

She sells herself for opera. She's a Vatican floozie.

They kiss in the bushes here. And the bushes are tubby
shirtless white guys playing bad guitar. Bad Grateful Dead
guitar, which is the deepest Hell for serious lovers.

I think Dyed Stitches is doing very good business.
  Can't talk too much to customers though while they're
shopping.
  No time for outward expression of inward grace.
  Never profitable.

They hate you if you show how truly happy you are.

Catch phrases:
Get Drunk Dyed Stitches
Hippie Camo (Dan's thought)

[Insert of Jill typing. Left out for copyright reasons]

There are so many showers need to be taken tonight. That's a lot
of water. I won't even try to imagine all the tub drains of August hippies.

I am not aloof. A shy guy who reacts nasty isn't afraid of people as much as he is disgusted by their scorn of the Golden Rule.

The virtues of a man skort for grilling.
Dan needs an orange to hide in his skort.

[Another Jill insert]

Jill can't outtype the misanthrope.

To think that there are only two sexes on earth pasting this circus together.
That's quite a lot of saliva glue.

Oh no, time for surrealism...
Bells and chocolate! There were three squirrels in the park foraging for nuts. A Catholic, Jew and Hindu squirrel.
The Catholic squirrel was asked what he intended to do with his nut.
"Bury it with my guilt," he confessed.
And the Jewish squirrel?
"Invest in my nephew's nutbutter factory in Hoboken."
And the Hindu?
"Certainly not roll pennies across a blue duck's bill!"

I told you this was surrealism.
Monkey's lips with vermilion tush.

Elephants speak for peanuts.
I still love you Rose.
A guy comes by to high five Rose.
She obliges.
Ron tells her to wash her hands, there might be LSD
residue to osmosify.
Paranoid tool I am.

You know you're getting old when you can't even pretend
that you don't want the rain to wash out your day in the sun.

Finally,
How many Dead Heads does it take to fill your typical in
ground pool with beer pee?

17.
and,

A box of wood for Jill from an admirer.
Jill: cellulose harlot.

One attractive-looking sock for the Ruby Slipper

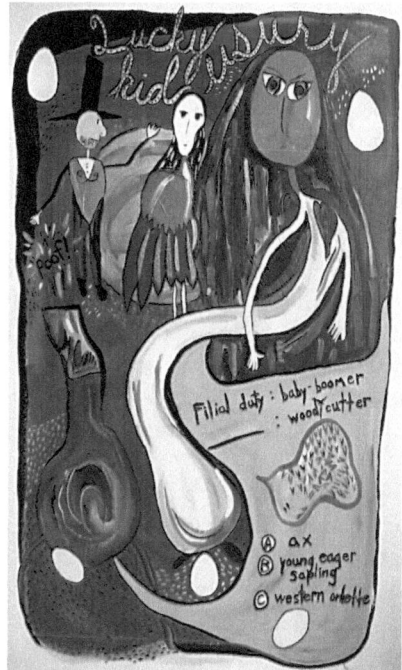

Lucky Kid Usury. 2009.
Acrylic on paper, 22 × 15"

I Don't Wanna Grow Up

Above is the reason the roast chicken becomes practically tasteless to couples who got into cohabiting and then debt without poetry.

Below is a statement of love that must be framed in the dooryard of any home lucky to stand in an overflowing economy.

August 1995

"Rose, today I set up my new home. You stopped by unexpectedly to be with me. You sat at my table scribbling notes while dipping torn chunks of bread in the minestrone. If you could taste what my eyes were saying you would hear in the sound of our lips smacking, all that was ever desired of the new century by man and woman. I am amazed. In the puff of my cheeks lives a soft pain that lasts day into night into day. A pain keeping me from sleep while I sleep. A pain of love. Rose.

I am having cheek dreams, wonderful and new. So new, right? And we have barely know each other!

You are the pain. You knock at my hovel door and immediately I begin missing you. I have this uncommon sense of immediacy. I must say this now before they come and ruin it all. I must tell you this without doubt before they come out of the rain and pound down my door. I must tell you right here and now, before the hands strike the hour when I will begin missing you for the rest of my life...

Miss Rose G. I love you. I love you. And one more time for the memory of our unborn children (because they're going to ignite everything meaningful to this moment anyway), I love you.

Now to let their fire burn us alive, after stuffing our socks with brimstone and coating our sheets in black powder. I have said it and meant it with a full heart. In the frame of a minute's eternity, any ocean of lighter fluid with accompanying mountain of TNT cannot stop me from loving you."

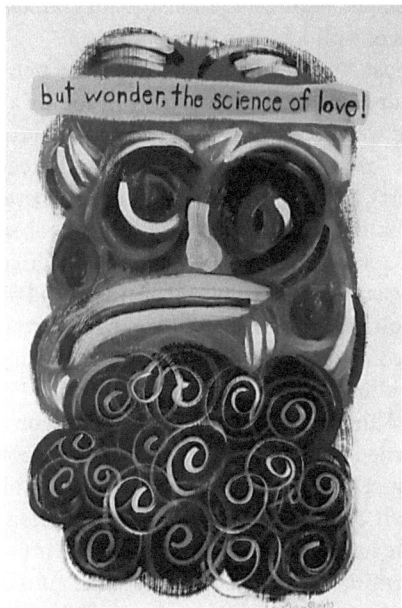

But Wonder, the Science of Love! 2013.
Acrylic on paper, 20 x 13"

The Second Amendment During Slavery Times

Let us secure weapons for protection. Rope? Spade shovel?
Wasp spray? No, no, we can have more formidable arms, says my
friend the science teacher, who is almost anti-gun. Rick mocks the
Second Amendment for its old-fashioned precepts with logic that
actually does quite well when run up against a fifteen foot thick
concrete wall partition. Like any proud American he wants to
protect our right to possess a firearm, but, wink-wink, it has to be
state-of-the-art, circa 1789. A front-loading musket with powder
flask and horn. He suggests even a brace of pistols, for those with
smaller balls but bigger families. We can sing Hallelujah, and

reload during a commercial break as some pimpled eighteen-year-old government assassin anonymously wipes out our entire street with the press of a pink button.

Rick, like most Americans, could really use a non-official history lesson. A lecture outside the mainstream. Not the kind where things are bad way back when, (enter the power-brokers), and then they're better, (because of power-brokers), and then better still, (power-brokers), better, (power-brokers again), better and better, (ditto), and finally the best Oceania will ever be. I would argue that the redcoats and the rebels of Colonial America were equally armed. So it was tit-for-tat time and again up and down the forest continent. "You gangrene me, and I'll gangrene you." A fairness in warfare existed where an artillery advantage was met with a shoot-'em and run military strategy. After the *Treaty of Paris* left parliament and the King wanting for cash, the people on the American continent learned first hand what happens when governments balloon into vast Empires. They get a bit unruly and disrespectful toward their constituents. Hence the Revolution and a bruise to Empire. The new Americans would keep their power-brokers in check by arming the people with the same guns Sam Adams greased down by the light of his kitchen fire. They would keep a militia, just like the modern Swiss do, only it would be mandated as a right, not a conscription.

I actually agree with Rick on the notion of the level playing field. One bullet for each gun, but all guns I say, especially the Empire's military guns. The redcoats and the rebels were equally armed with the same technology. General Howe had a bigger arsenal, so Washington kept better maps of the trees and rocks. Rapes and looting occurred for sure, but had to be the exception in a land where Johnny, the cooper's boy, knew how to load a Bess and hide out in the hog barn.

But this reasoning just confirms the gross limitations of my modern-day pot-bellied politics. Broad access to technological advancements in 18th century weaponry equalized the people and their government. The Second Amendment guaranteed that cooperation, and not coercion, would settle differences. It was a radical realism at the time, marked along with several other precepts that would insure power to, well, some of the people anyway. Enough to keep the government weary of the mental health of the majority of its citizens. Same would be for today if the industrial revolution did not warp the playing field to such a monstrously, gross imbalance. Of course there is always the chance that China would fry us all on a stick tomorrow, if the United States, got so ill-logical that it voted to rid the earth of its own participation in global mega-violence, by disbanding the military, smelting all weaponry, and re-arming the populace with muzzle loaders. Then again, maybe not. For who has China engaged militarily since its revolution? Besides reacting to westerners invading Korea and millions of its own helpless people?

The point I need to make to Rick is that the arsenals of our military brass are stocked to the stratosphere with post-modern psychotic weapons of the apocalypse. That the FBI, CIA, ATF, Homeland Security, the Secret Service, private bodyguards of Michael Bloomberg and every gas company CEO, that is, all government agencies and cold, corporate lobbies, are packing enough heat to shred our kids bodies to oblivion. If one day Rick wakes up born again American revolutionary, and drools all "crazy constitutional", perhaps even yearning to worship the tobacco seeds I shared with him this spring, and organizes a wild powwow with the sacred herb and other peoples of like mind to sing lustily of his new found freedom, the uninvited ATF and FBI can surround his house with flamethrowers to call him out. If Rick questions their trespass, (he might have the gall to declare to the government thugs that the barrel of a gun will never influence his politics), the bureau chief may suggest igniting the compound (his house) and shooting anything alive that falls out (his family and friends).

That is why good Americans defend the second amendment. Personally I have no desire to possess more than a musket in my arsenal. And I would call out every good citizen to accept similar equalization, to empower us all. But what use while just one of our Marine companies can boast of a grenade launcher tossing four hundred bombs per second into a crowd of politically incorrect humane life? They have the machine on display at the State Fair this Labor Day. I would dare Rick to stand before it to test each of the first ten amendments that he heard about once or twice in grade school, and maybe on and off for half a year in a civics elective in one of the upper grades. Be creative Rick. Wear a turban on your head. Carry a copy of an imam-inscribed Koran up to Sergeant Sociopath of Company C. Turn, and begin handing out leaflets which highlight the virtues of *Das Capital*. Chant the mantra "Our President is a fascist Mussolini killing brown babies like a sissy-coward ", or something along those lines. Stuff bags of oregano in your sleeves, Give a PDA to a willing man beside you. Overall, just keep up the good work of expressing the rights your country provided to you at birth. Then during a brief lapse in this show, in a non-threatening manner, expose your brace of pistols attached at the hip.

What will happen to you Rick?

The question must be, "Why would anything happen to you Rick in a free society?"

Apprehension is our present mental state. Because just imagining public expression of our rights puts the fear of naked death into us foolish little boys and girls.

So some of us have access to our pop guns. Creatively used, if necessary, could pick off one or two oil spill CEOs, just to begin a reconnection of Golden Rule neurons back into our central nervous systems. For to think that their right to life is equal unto ours, even after people explode apart, and millions of gallons of oil gush into the sea, upsetting the natural balance of ten thousand years—if just one man, one BP executive, has the power to fling the backs of his fingers across his chin at a million suffering species, including the last living representation of mankind, and yet not spend even an overnight in a Mississippi county jail cell, then Rick and I, and especially all hominids inhabiting the gulf coast, worship true power over any fictitious god, as well as our wives, children, mothers, fathers sisters, brothers included. We fear power with a gusto that devours brotherly love.

Yes, it's depressing. A German nation 70 years back would agree. Whether its sixty or three hundred million, obedience wrought by fear trumps truth and buries justice every time. Still Rick, the Second Amendment guarantees at least a mild retaliation for us Winston Smiths of the present and future.

I am keeping my pop-gun oiled.

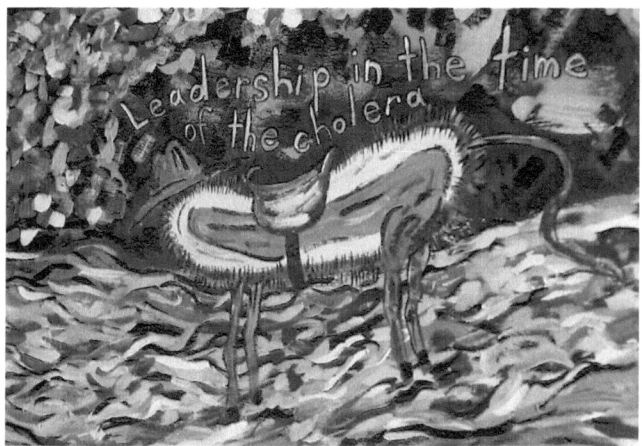

From *Panem et Circenses*. 2013. Acrylic on old secretary with homemade country wines and other stuff. 60 x 24 x 20"

Hydrofracking Anti-work

The fact that a 46 year old man, simple, shy and nearly as honest as his neighbor ever was, feels the need to take up what the elites of my state are claiming is a cause célebre over the pros and cons of chemically infecting our water supply, is a sign of the black SUV times.

Even our local "public" radio is in on the money game, selling advertising to the gas men who espouse child leukemia as a justifiable result of fake farmer Fred's purchase of a speed boat to play with while the subsidized high fructose corn syrup grows tall.

The governor is corrupt, his friends all greed punks, his girlfriend a very bad human being, and not even a good cook, really. Phenol crab cakes. A mixed green salad washed in naphthalene. A glass of formaldehyde Finger Lakes wine delivered to her door by the sleazy state senator who dreams paper money is happiness.

It amazes me that these lawyer-cowards are not hanging from a stick, by a thread, over a frack pool bubbling with mass community rage.

Stanley Milgram would have nodded his head while the people of the village turn the voltage up on their own screaming children.

So I take up paint and mix in what I think is the second most audacious power grab ever made by human beings. The first being the advent of probable nuclear annihilation by future lawyer-cowards. My neighbors watch and listen to the fake debate and wait to judge which side the hippies fall on. They all love CSN, and even Neil Young before he broke away and wrote the poetry of a grown-up. They just don't appreciate hippies bearing a conscience. All are waiting for the lawyer-cowards to set up the tent of the crazy circus debate on hydrofracking. And established tools like my local public radio people perpetuate the power grab with credit card payment glee. They don't need to be millionaires. They all just want to look like one.

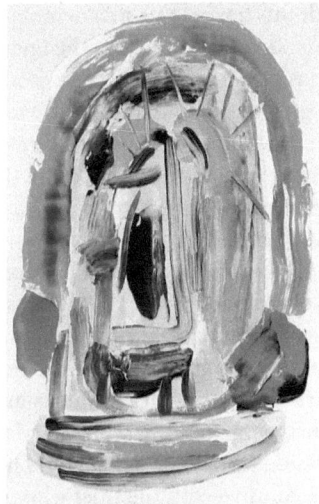

Summer Circus Clown 1862. 2013.
Acrylic on paper, 15 x 7"

Ancient Quote From Bacterial Frenchman

I keep wondering how normal people cope so well with
Hoover-esque sociopaths monitoring our cyber activity.

I believe in the power of antibiotics. The greatest wonder of scientific evolution. Lives are saved every day thanks to a progressive
march toward human betterment in science. I wonder, though, if
political evolution hit a brick wall 500 years ago. Maybe all culture
need not be progressive.

"Poor, wretched, and stupid peoples, nations determined on your
own misfortune and blind to your own good! You let yourselves be
deprived before your own eyes of the best part of your revenues;
your fields are plundered, your homes robbed, your family heir-
looms taken away. You live in such a way that you cannot claim
a single thing as your own; and it would seem that you consider

yourselves lucky to be loaned your property, your families, and your very lives. All this havoc, this misfortune, this ruin, descends upon you not from alien foes, but from the one enemy whom you yourselves render as powerful as he is, for whom you go bravely to war, for whose greatness you do not refuse to offer your own bodies unto death. He who thus domineers over you has only two eyes, only two hands, only one body, no more than is possessed by the least man among the infinite numbers dwelling in your cities; he has indeed nothing more than the power that you confer upon him to destroy you. Where has he acquired enough eyes to spy upon you, if you do not provide them yourselves? How can he have so many arms to beat you with, if he does not borrow them from you? The feet that trample down your cities, where does he get them if they are not your own? How does he have any power over you except through you? How would he dare assail you if he had no cooperation from you? What could he do to you if you yourselves did not connive with the thief who plunders you, if you were not accomplices of the murderer who kills you, if you were not traitors to yourselves? You sow your crops in order that he may ravage them, you install and furnish your homes to give him goods to pillage; you rear your daughters that he may gratify his lust; you bring up your children in order that he may confer upon them the greatest privilege he knows— to be led into his battles, to be delivered to butchery, to be made the servants of his greed and the instruments of his vengeance; you yield your bodies unto hard labor in order that he may indulge in his delights and wallow in his filthy pleasures; you weaken yourselves in order to make him the stronger and the mightier to hold you in check. From all these indignities, such as the very beasts of the field would not endure, you can deliver yourselves if you try, not by taking action, but merely by willing to be free. Resolve to serve no more, and you are at once freed. I do not ask that you place hands upon the tyrant to topple him over, but simply that you support him no longer; then you will behold him, like a great Colossus whose pedestal has been pulled away, fall of his own weight and break in pieces."

—Étienne de la Boétie

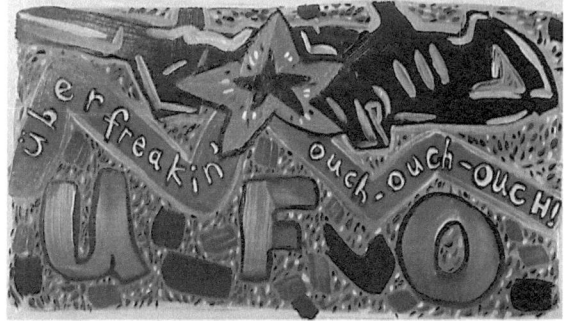

U.F.O. 2012. Acrylic on paper, 15 x 7"

Edward Snowden Funny Comic Strip

So few moments in my lifetime where I can laugh out loud at the secret torturers.

He's getting away! Take that you slavering Berlusconi knee-spanking bankers! Ha-ha-ha.

Still, I know that this sweet irony cannot last too long. The surveillance state getting made a fool of by Winston Smith will not be tolerated. If they can't catch him tonight, our paid for goons will torture the poor man's grandmother with a spiny lizard or coffee spoon. Mr. Snowden has the multi-billion dollar super-sissy infrastructure wetting its pants in international embarrassment. Like I was telling my wife this morning... These men and women running the power structure are our contemporaries. They are not more educated, more qualified, more of any thing that you and I are not. They are the über-rich, who do not like to follow the law when it blocks the delivery of their über riches. For that they need control. It worked for eleven years of box-cutter fears. Yet babies keep getting born and most of the human world, I believe, getting better behaved.

Not in our neck of the woods, however. I believe we would all benefit if our crime bosses had the Constitution paper cut into their eyeballs.

My grandfather fought in World War II for these lickspittle senators and congressmen? My father's friends fought and died in Vietnam to perpetuate frauds and murderers like Donald Rumsfeld and Barack Obama?

Ho boy! The world is changing fast. Now Ecuador appears to be the safe haven for political dissidents. This is good. Too good to be truly happening. Enjoy your Internet now my fellow Chinamen. The central authority at centcom of the homeland will be turning out the lights before you can say "We the people..."

And...

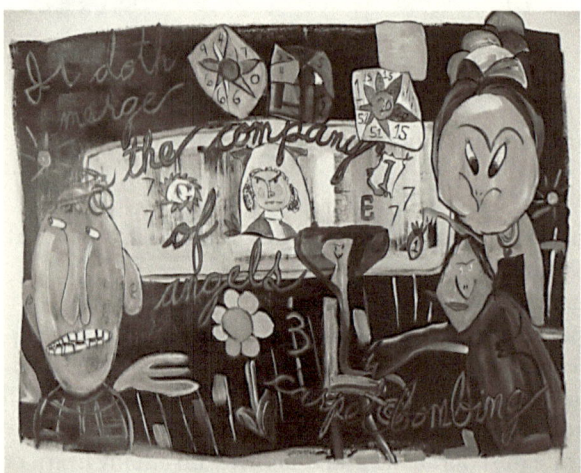

Good Company. 2008. Acrylic on paper, 18 x 25"

An extraordinary day in the life of man-as-individual-conscience-stricken-moral-animal vs. mafia bulldogs on crack jag of grandeur delusion. We are witnessing an act of war taking place. World war initiated by the present Washington goons prostituting for financial mullahs. They plan world design religiously while underground like an evil Batman in a billionaire's cave.

This supreme arrogance must be washed away quickly. It is all too obvious that the United States is now pariah. To not let Evo Morales travel through French or Portuguese airspace on the grounds that he may be harboring an unarmed creature seeking political asylum, one who brings on board no more wealth than the 50 cents of elemental worth that make up his four cubic feet of flesh, is a piratical high crime on the air seas. Pariah Austria too harboring a totalitarian government that searches a presidential plane for a skinny kid with nothing more than information about a bunch of dirty perverts peeping in on the world's toilets.

The pariah comfort jocks of any village who pretend to believe in honesty and justice, but really just want to look good for the committee, must be feeling a bit of pressure. They react.

And my local public radio diligently obeys, hosting the propaganda 24/7, as if the Internet did not exist to trump their faux news on every play. Tom Paine now informs any house on the street who seeks Tom Paine.

To think we have a President, Congress, and Judiciary, three branches of the government tree, steadfastly working to defend and protect that quaint document written by slaveholders and other suspect old men. Gay marriage *is* nice. Guns *can* be scary. Immigration *should* be reformed. But all progress is meaningless if a gay Mexican lady shouldering a Bushmaster has the Bill of Rights stuffed down her throat and is made to ride shotgun beside an investigative journalist whose Mercedes-Benz is hot rigged to crash and burn.

Oh well. Read Kenneth Patchen:

The birds are very careful of this world
Ha! a lot of good
that'll do them!
(Behind those desks
some mighty
dangerous guys
are sitting, baby.)

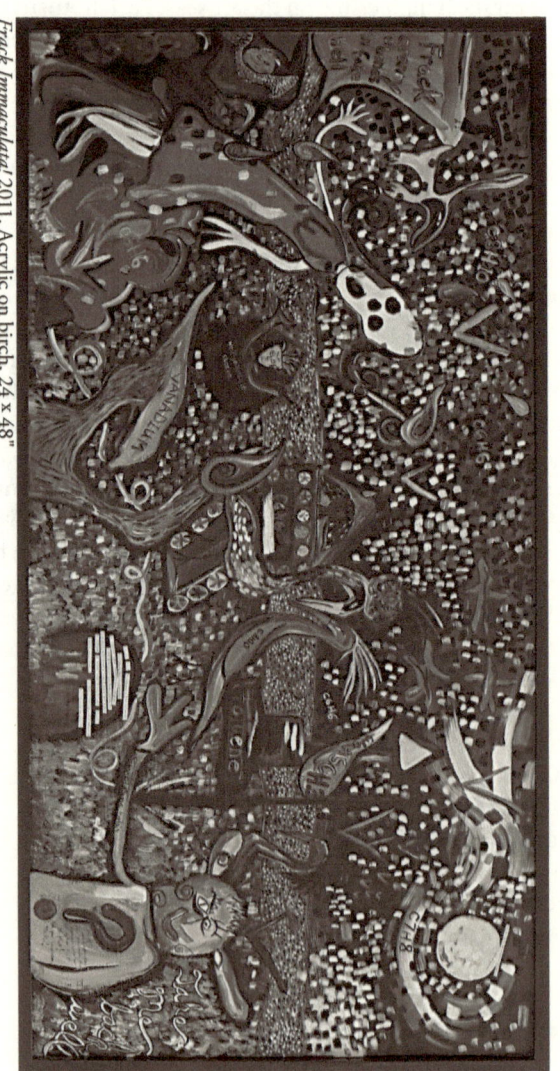

Frack Immaculata! 2011. Acrylic on birch, 24 x 48"

My Speech to the Basement Glass of Wine

I am taking art to the level it was meant to be. Presently I am documenting our last battle.

I am one man, one artist insane, crazy enough to place the entire hydro-fracking debate onto my shoulders. I have taken up a position, and now will give the only argument morally acceptable. I shall schlop onto canvas, paper, and hardboard the property rapists of my country in all the colors of their inside organs and respective juices. After viewing my show, all pro-fracking dreams will blow out of the state quicker than the greedy ass-crack stampede from Texas that brought them here.

I shall not take up a scientific argument on the process. Hydraulic fracturing of the Marcellus Shale has the potential of poisoning the groundwater for hundreds of thousands of people for many generations. A man need only hear this news once to react. Even if there isn't a bit of truth to it. Just using the logic of foraging black bears would measure some intelligent questions to follow. Who is to profit from these drilling ventures? Is it true that there are cases where tap water out west can be ignited from a faucet? What are the chemicals used in the process? Why doesn't the industry have to disclose them publicly? Pushing millions of gallons of freshwater laced with up to a hundred chemicals (known and unknown) into the rock bed under high pressure to release mass quantities of methane just doesn't sound that safe, does it? I mean, even to a moron, or an alcoholic, or wife beater. So why does the Governor of New York State allow this kind of Texas oilman trespass upon his constituents? True, the silent-majority of Americans are mostly short-sighted, greedy, selfish thugs, always ready with an opinion on either side of the death debate. Farmer Ted: "A hundred grand a lease? That's powerful money. I don't want government telling me who not to poison. Where do I sign?"

Governor Andrew: "Eight million to my super PAC? Screw New York infants!"

I am working on a painting to shame the governor out of his fine Italian suit. I have the bones of his grandmother, Immaculata, in a red dress, being shot from her Long Island grave by a geyser of liquid carcinogens. Some shore birds and other funny creatures are hanging out in the cemetery on a moonlit night. Words across the sky might read: *Hey Governor, We Sure Hope That Immaculata Isn't Fracked Out of the Very Ground You Saturate With Poison.* We'll see what kind of reaction I get from our state boss. I will put on a price tag of six thousand dollars. Maybe he will buy it to destroy it. Half of the proceeds will pay my tax to the Onondaga. The other half will go toward a bigger painting of shame until the Governor uses his overpaid trooper skirts to escort Texas oil the hell off our land.

Laissez-faire capitalism was a grand party for the chosen few during the 19th century. And it ran like a top beside the presence of cholera and death-by-childbirth. Such frequent miseries kept all survival joys in check. A slave workforce made anyone not a slave much too busy to oversee the rich neighbor's trespass. And the water was always dirty poop, for science had not yet escaped the confines of the Pentateuch. God took little Johnny because it was predestined to be. What matter that Grandma picked pole beans with fecal fingers? Or that they laid Johnny to rest with his lead toy soldier ten feet from the well-sweep? Suzy was next, and the family watched her every move with working dread.

Today we know better. We know a lot about the environment and the fragile balance that exists wherever man settles his toxic prejudice. Modern families don't pour known carcinogens into their wells for a paycheck. Yet for some wicked reason the government by the people, and for the people, wants to persuade the people to consider this action as an economic opportunity. Poison our kids and we will reap wonderful financial benefits. Instant winnings for the well leasers. Trickle-down, cheap energy for everyone else. A few, maybe even thirty dead kids, but all iPhones still humming at Cafe des Artistes on the Upper West Side.

Politics have officially warped into a vile adjunct of corporate power. The Governor knows hydrofracking has the potential to make all life around it sick and dying. He knows that the majority of his lunch friends are corrupt, negligent, and possibly homicidal in their dealings with the red-faced Texans and their high greed agenda. Yet he still touts childhood cancer as a regretful, albeit necessary result of hydraulic fracturing.

We who matter should have our legs sawed off for being such

cowards. Why is my call for immediate arrest of the Governor ignored? He should be unkindly imprisoned for life for perpetuating this phony debate endangering the better health of our friends and families.

Another angle to consider is this: New York State government has no authority to offer these carpetbagging cheese faces high bid rights to our land. The chemical water shoots over boundaries, and seeps across roads.

It's a vote of no-confidence folks. Take a walk in the woods to reflect upon who has power over your family and friends. I shall start paying my tax to the true nation-state where throughout this life I rest my travel bones. The Onondaga base their policy decisions on how the seventh generation will be affected. Oh that is wise. And strong. The Governor could use a real father-chief to slap him down in shame before the rest of the tribe.

The dumb among us will take all of their neighbors to the justice of the Onondaga quicker than a frack-gush up the proverbial coke nose of avarice

We are so poisoned in the brain by this government we prop up by virtue of a coddled economy.

Here's a take from a long dead Atlantic traveler on how man has become a somewhat useful pawn of the present state:

After having thus successively taken each member of the community in its powerful grasp and fashioned him at will, the supreme power then extends its arm over the whole community. It covers the surface of society with a network of small complicated rules, minute and uniform, through which the most original minds and the most energetic characters cannot penetrate, to rise above the crowd. The will of man is not shattered, but softened, bent, and guided; men are seldom forced by it to act, but they are constantly restrained from acting. Such a power does not destroy, but it prevents existence; it does not tyrannize, but it compresses, enervates, extinguishes, and stupefies a people, till each nation is reduced to nothing better than a flock of timid and industrious animals, of which the government is the shepherd.
—de Tocqueville

Those local clans still bearing a conscience need to organize a mob. The land men want your land. The companies they represent want to see your babies get sick for a profit. A super biggie profit. A hot dangy-dong-diddle-dee-doo kind of big fat Texas goo profit. A glass of cool, fresh Indian water and not-so-indian carcinogenic compounds to quench a summer thirst. A Saturday night bath and a red rash tattoo for little coughing Tom and coffin Sue. What's it worth to you, shale squatters of the present moment? A temporary new smell in a shiny red pick-up? A pole barn envy? The NFL Sunday ticket?

They desire a hot ejaculation of benzene and phenol into your village groundwater. The Governor hovers above in a trooper chopper, rubbing his hands together in a show of fiendish glee. He longs to see all of you rurals heaped onto a pile. Your pathetic firehouse vote is laughable to the millions of Manahattas sucking the earth out from under your feet. A hundred grand to sicken my family for life? Really? That much, eh?

Okay, I'm in. Wait till they see my loaded Deere at the Grange. That hog Harold Hoenow will be green from envy, and that Vanadium cocktail he shared on the porch with Ruth.

No, I have to hope there is still a slurry of indigenous righteousness left swirling in our guts. Please good people temporarily living atop the ancient beds of shale, be kind and hospitable to the landmen at your door. A smile and a kind word is all anybody needs. And on a hot summer's day, a cold glass of lemon-lime aid sweetened with antifreeze wouldn't hurt either. It might teach these raunchy carpetbaggers to prey on their own kind back in the dumbed-down, drought-dried southlands.

They're coming to a door near you. Get 'em.

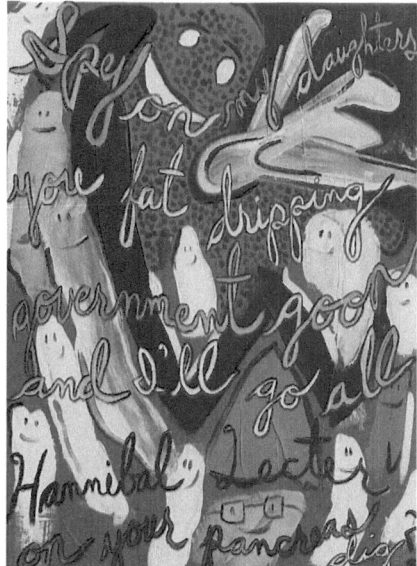

Spy on My Daughters You Fat Dripping Govern-
ment Goon and I'll Go All Hannibal Lecter on Your
Pancreas, Dig? 2013. Acrylic on canvas, 24 x 18"

Homeland

I don't want to discuss it. If our leaders are not in prison by the end of the year, then the United States my great-great-grandfather knew, the one who burned up all the tepees across the plains of Crazy Horse, has officially warped into a post modern fascist state of ultra-secretive cyber-wussies.

Homeland! What kind of a word is that you McDonald's Coca-Cola-Googlemart freaks of anti-nature? Do the lot of you propagandist nannies truly think that word stirs the patriotic flagella of the dumbed down masses? Both the millionaire senator and White House podium have uttered the Hitler word in the last 24 hours. Times up. They are too desperate to lead effectually. Take them back to Bavaria and strip them down behind a fence before it's too late.

Homeland! My leaders are so stinking dirty.

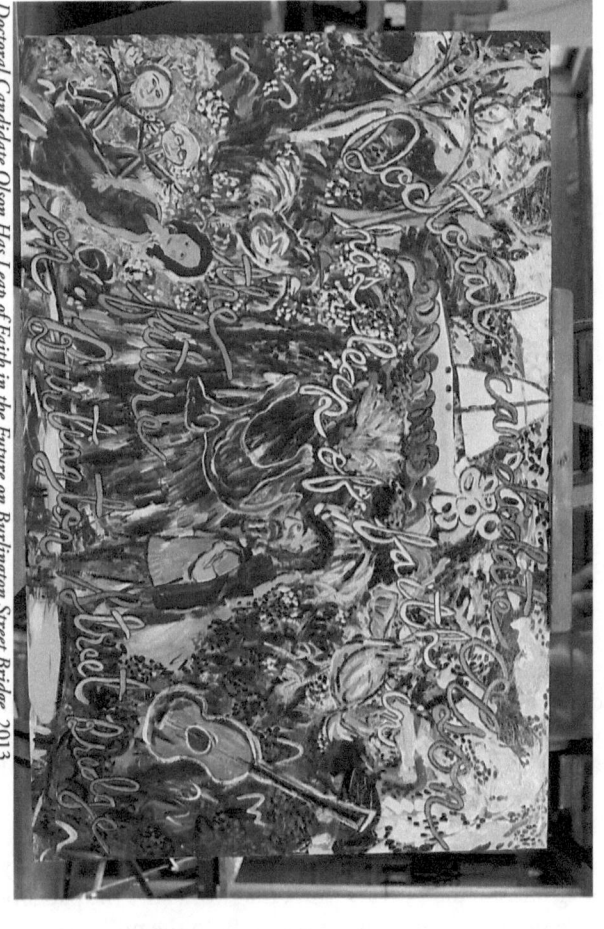

Doctoral Candidate Olson Has Leap of Faith in the Future on Burlington Street Bridge. 2013. Acrylic on panelboard, 32 x 48".

My Friend the Doctor

Here is a work that John Lennon would relate to if he played mind games without the promise of unending royalties delivered to Beatles Inc. Which man knows where he will be in twenty years? I made it simple for myself back in '93 and '94. A soup on the stove at fifty. Steamed corn on a plate and a sense of humor. I am still waiting and working for that day to come. I set my standards low and thus have achieved more than I ever dreamed, so far.

My friend in the painting has a Sumerian look to him. His eye(s) are set on the prize. Fleeting future dreams of a family—his girlfriend-to-be-wife, children, a dog, free use of a guitar, sailing vessel, sculptural wonders, and chickens in the yard. Who knew? Like me he could have ended up dropping fries at a truck stop off Interstate 65. Also, like me, he works to dream, and gets more kick out of life than any Beatle writing candy songs. That is "the meaning of success", some reformed millionaire heroin addict could only dream about.

The painting is a gift for you and the wife professor. I know it is loud and there might not be a place for it in the most prominent living spaces of the house. Relegated to the garage wall or a ceiling space in the attic would not offend me in the least. Consider this a protocol from the unconfident American artist. If you accept the work, leave a dozen eggs by the door this week, and be done with it. Give me a few days first to frame it.

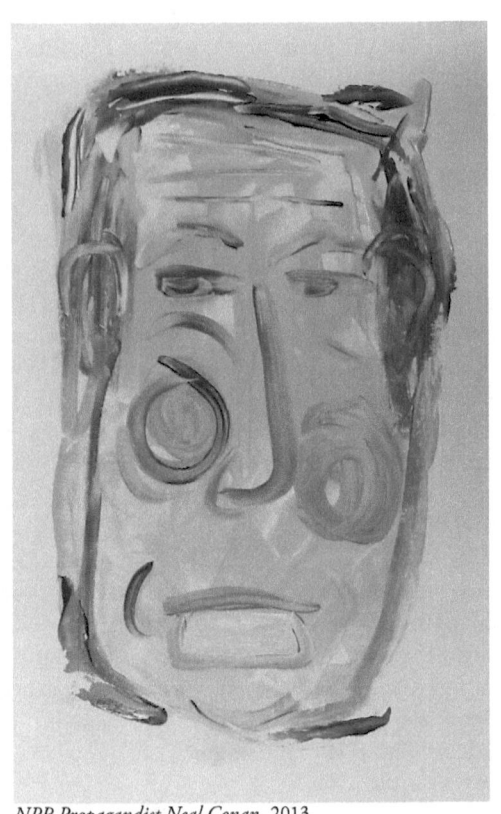

NPR Propagandist Neal Conan. 2013.
Acrylic on paper, 16 x 7"

Iran War Studies

Here we go again. Israel is telling our people to hurry along now. For one hour during my ride back home I listened to a coven of National Propaganda witches tongue dancing proof of why each is more educated by avarice than the other. And their subject of discussion? The life and death of children 5,000 miles away. One of the guests (nearly always a professor from Georgetown or a New York Times "reporter") actually said our east coast is vulnerable to Nuclear attack. He knows that public opinion will always be in favor of killing if it is afraid, and the new world media thugs sell fear very well.

He knows too that Iran is surrounded, and that just an aggressive launch of a flaming Ho-Ho from the Ayatollah will render each and every Iranian city a smoking death valley. He is certain that Neal Conan will not ask about Israel's nuclear arsenal, nor remind him of the only wild west country to melt other people's babies with nuclear weapons. The guests tacitly agree that Neal is a killer by association. A war propagandist. And they don't care. Which means in my sincere artist opinion that they want to melt babies. They talk about war or no war like deciding on the purchase of French cheese at the supermarket.

I hate them. They are smart cowards. Their lives are secure and they know it. They can say anything. They can spout death. Not only do they fill up their grocery cart with imported goodies, but they buy the whole wheel of French cheese.

These paintings are about the coming slaughter of innocents.

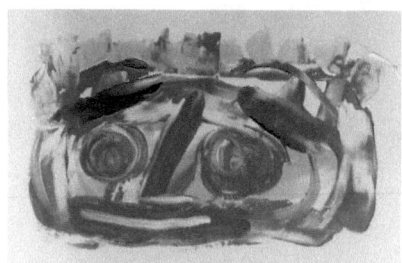

A Tel Aviv Hooker. 2013.
Acrylic on paper, 8 x 17

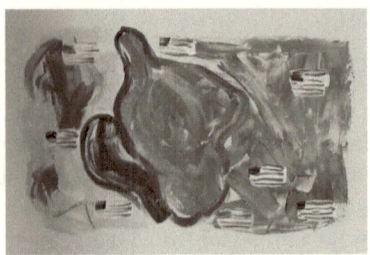

Special Senate Committee Document Proving Iran is Surrounded and Therefore Quite Able to Murder Us All in Our Sleep. 2013. Acrylic on paper, 7 x 15"

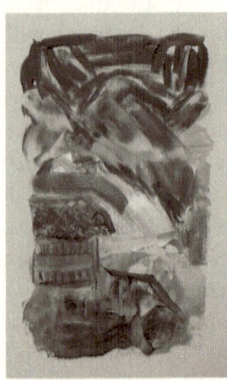

Private Push-button Takes Wife to Ruby Tuesday's After Fierce Drone Battle With Unarmed Family in Tehran Compound. 2013. Acrylic on paper, 16 x 7"

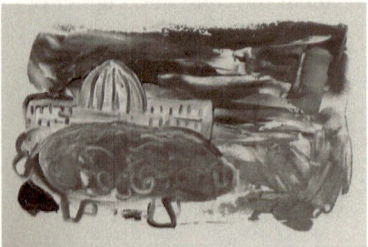

Free Pork Lunch for Lawyer Congressmen. 2013. Acrylic on paper, 7 x 15"

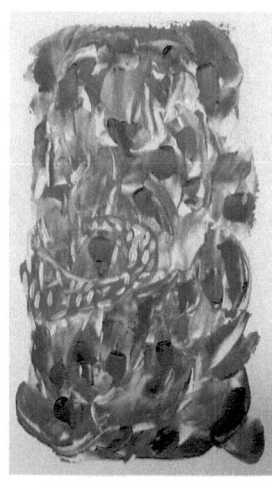

*East Coast Obliterated by
Nuclear Weapon Sent Via
Souped-up Amphibious
Paykan Van.* 2013.
Acrylic on paper, 16 x 7"

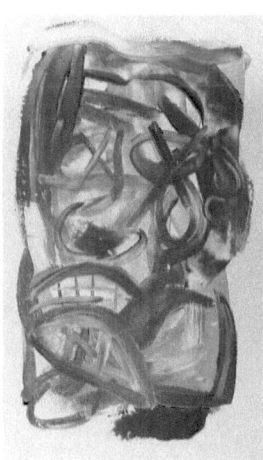

*Private Push-button's Heart
Attack at the Taco Bell.* 2013.
Acrylic on paper, 15 x 7"

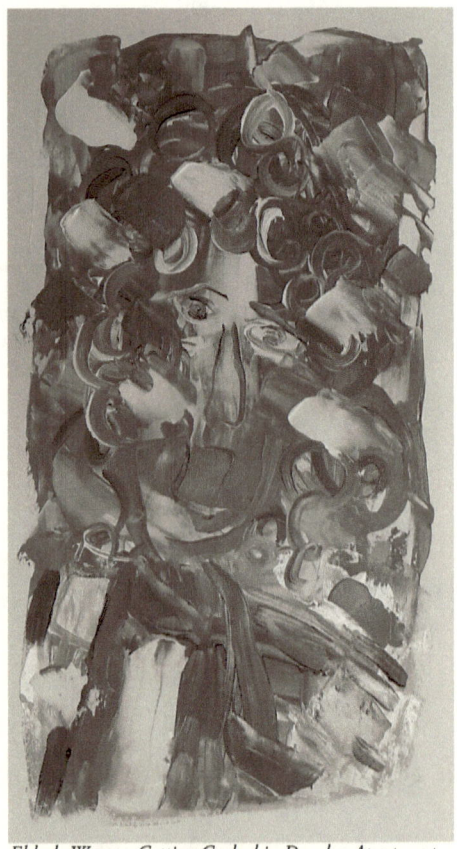

Elderly Woman Getting Cooked in Dresden Apartment.
2013. Acrylic on paper, 17 x 8"

World War II Studies

More war stories. I think I'll call it "The Lucky Seven". At 7:00 p.m. I descend into my studio and paint seven stories onto printing press clean-up sheets. The "lucky" are those fortunate to have lived during wartime when fear gathered all the people together in violence and racism.

World History is every class necessary to earn a degree in group psychology. Groupthink is an oxymoron, and a fear that consumes me with its mighty power. Just a brief read in any LIFE magazine published during the war years to see my point.

Can propaganda alone sway public opinion? Is the latter anything that the most noise (visual and official) says it is?

I think so.

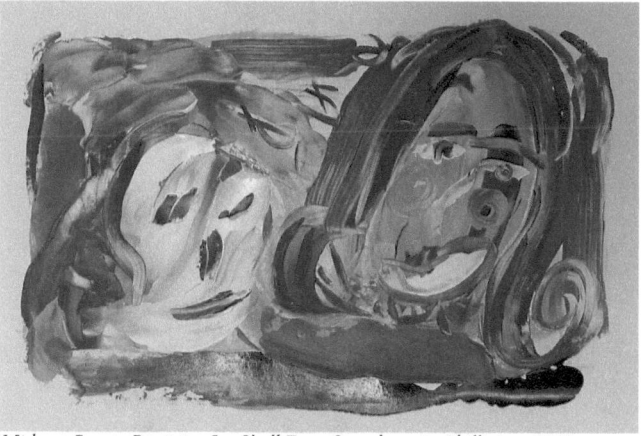

Midwest Beauty Receiving Jap Skull From Sweetheart in Phillipines. 2013.
Acrylic on paper, 8 x 17"

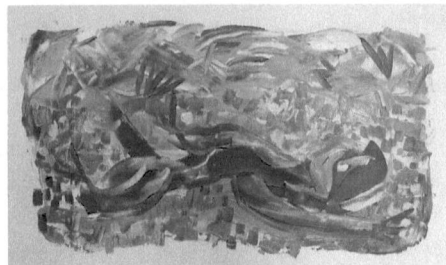

Russian Socialist Farmer Thawing in Spring Flowers.
2013. Acrylic on paper, 7 x 16"

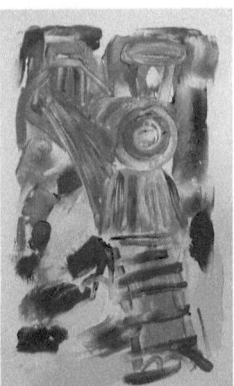

Train Track to Auschwitz
Unmolested. 2013.
Acrylic on paper, 16 x 7"

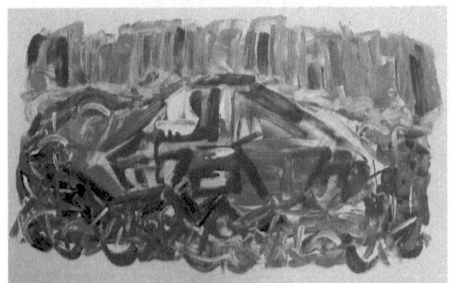

Amphibious Vehicle Adding to Aquatic Din at Omaha
Beach. 2013. Acrylic on paper, 7 x 15"

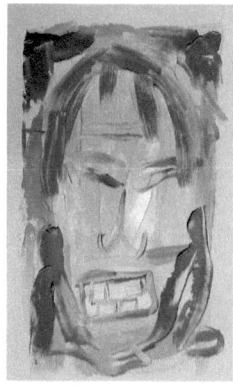

*Ralph the U.S. Citizen
Holding the Fence at
Manzanar.* 2013.
Acrylic on paper, 15 x 7"

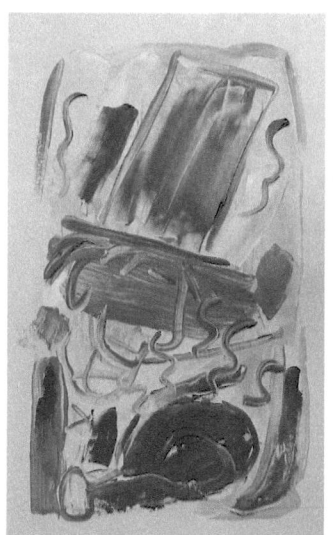

President Kill and the Roast Turkey.
2013. Acrylic on paper, 16 x 7"

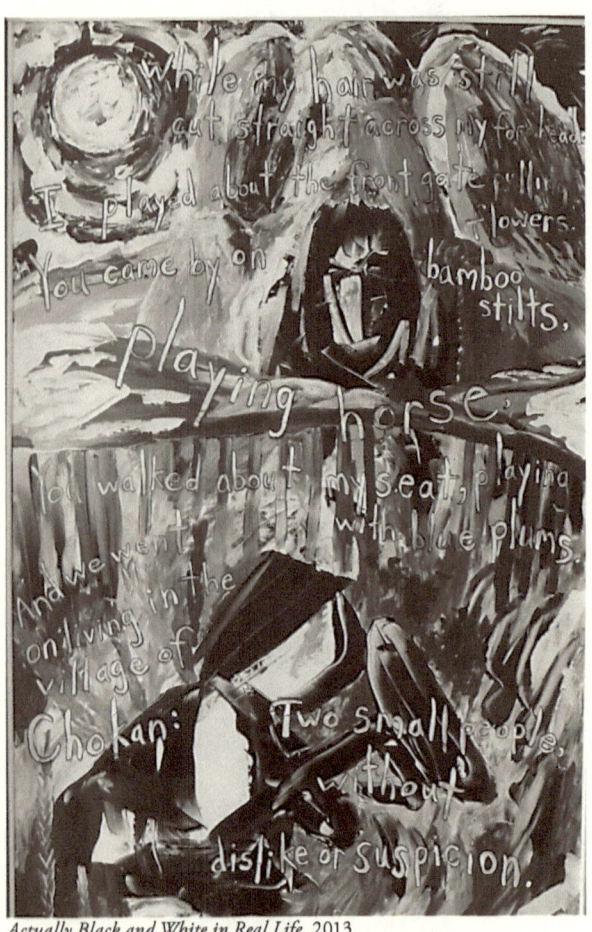

Actually Black and White in Real Life. 2013.
Acrylic on panelboard, 48 × 32"

April is Clean Up Time With Paints, Squeezing Out Tubes, and Making History

For me freedom happens whenever I am arrested by the element X. Yesterday's work was spent dreaming about what will be if I allow the X in for longer periods of time. This isn't bragging or false modesty. It is what it is. I am an artist, good or bad, but one through and through. Yesterday I would have painted on the cats if there was no canvas or paper at hand. But then I read to my daughter, improvised a rich stew, painted frames, cleaned out cat litter boxes, made beds, did laundry, planted late garlic—basically chased the ten thousand things which all of us are bound to do.

But not once the money exchange.

As a younger man I should have had my fortune read to spare a future old man anguish. But then I never would have believed it. Now at 46, instead of the positive I-Ching thunder at the well, my "art" gets thrown down into the well. Financial success is not showing in any card, and I guess that was meant to be, for me.

Artists never wanted a built-in swimming pool with cocktails at sunset anyway. I can tell who the wealth-desiring phonies are from a gated community away. It's just that the onset of old age has me devaluing my efforts more often, when I know I should keep the fighting attitude alive and strong.

All of this is okay if viewed future-historically. I know the value of archiving struggle. *For posterity.* Today there is mostly some tall-order crap in galleries and museums. In New York, they take thirty percent of your skin (if you're lucky to get a foot in the door of four white walls and around-the-room track lighting) because the power of influencing rich stupid people is basically an art in itself. These liaisons play their part, maintaining personal wealth and status while courting filthy rich imbeciles of a lower order. But they only serve a present purpose, and much of that is made in the past. The art collectors have money. The artists do not. There has never been a time on earth when the latter held their heads financially high like bankers in Mercedes. Cave painters were probably tolerated their art for performing some other shameful, putrid tasks. Cleaning out the crap corner of the cave, or burying the six-day-old dead. The ones who stubbornly held their arms to the chest declaring "not another demeaning task," were probably tossed over the nearest cliff.

I am a cave painter in a poor upstate village. If there are three art buyers here, they have already cornered the market on still life apples and chiaroscuro candles melting wax. I have an existential-ist's chance in heaven to be supported by my community. Unless I decide to seek the Calvinistic retardation of "mop a floor for your dinner". Then I will be financially independent, and afford any smartphone with its two-year contract.

No. I have a rich wife who supports me because I support her.

And I see into the future an immense archive sold at auction for $500.00, with a U-Haul rental fee waived. My grandchildren will get an education in the arts, enough to know that dedication and devotion to painting, or the like, where there is no contemporary investment, is like mopping an institution's floors for free because you think you deserve the pool and cocktail-at-sunset prize, even though, after all, it was just a shiny floor. And nobody, not a single soul in your world, ever pressed you to live this fool's eternity.

P.S. Please feel free to share my work with a wealthy gallery renter in NYC. She can take 90% commission. I'll ask my friend Dan to load up his mini-van and we could be set up in a day. Tell her that I am handsome enough for my age, and on opening night would mousse my remaining hair and talk to prospective buyers as if they too possessed the artist's hopeful soul, and not the caged rabid animal gesticulating in their void. Tell her that I am more desperate than a dead Basquiat or a living pervert like Jeff Koons ever was. Tell her that if given a small financial push, the gigantic chip on my shoulder would explode in creativity, which could help her realize her dream: the pool and cocktail-at-sunset prize.

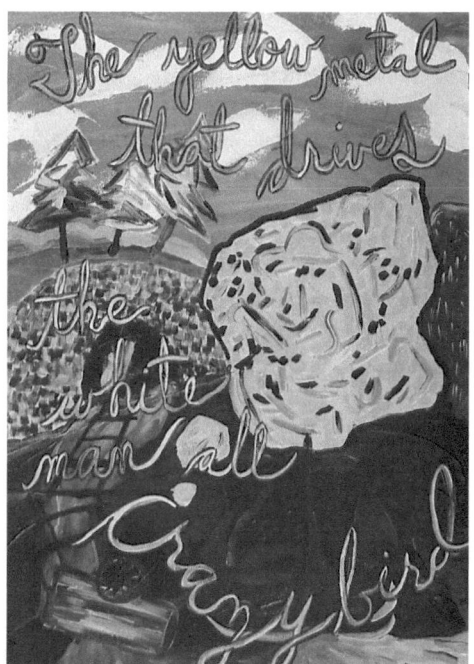

The Yellow Metal That Drives the White Man All Crazy Bird. 2013. Acrylic on canvas, 24 × 18"

Why Do I Always Have to Explain?

I get up in the morning and I get my brief
I stare out at the world in complete disbelief
It's not righteous indignation that makes me complain
It's the fact that I always have to explain.

—Van Morrison

Presently I am working on a painting of a gold nugget. I believe the 546 people who govern the 300,000,000 have gold nuggets for brains. I believe the departments and agencies that work alongside the 546 have black powder packed full into testicles and ovaries. They are friendly good fathers and mothers like the couple who raised today's flavor of serial killer.

There are about 26 million who depend on bid contracts from these departments and agencies. They are just scaredy-cats with car payments. I would be among these tools too with a coveted job at the Smithsonian or National Gallery. No doubt about it.

It's too early in the morning for me to break it down further. Plug in subsidized farming, fishing, meat-packing, oil-drilling, bomb-sniffing dog grooming, the entire state of Oklahoma, and the illegal immigrant future voting block of Tammany Hall desperation... to find everyone seated together on a bright afternoon at the Coliseum, or standing tree-side at a boredom-killing mob lynching of Indians in the new public square.

I have no fix today or any day.

Thank You Millions and Billions Who Came Before

A toast to medicine and bleach, antibiotics, cheap textiles, heated homes, affordable homes, homes with coffee makers, hot water, public sewers, septic technology, information sharing, inspected slaughterhouses, invisible farmers and harvesters, the automobile, electric light and power, men and women who accumulate knowledge in trade schools and universities, inventors, grocery and liquor stores, outdoor markets, well-known companies that create motors and metal alloys to stock our kitchens and laundry rooms. A toast to 11,000 years of post Ice Age innovation and unfortunate suffering to the multiple billions of my evolving brothers and sisters! It is time for me to thank the unlucky of yesteryear. This is it, this time and place, and some days it is too wonderful to look at.

Disclaimer: *I know it is power with its control of resources that raises my standard of living to the unbelievable. I know there are worlds still upon earth that suffer for my little joys and thankfulness. I can do what I can and hope the rest are able to claim some peaceful moments during their lives of toil and terror. For now, in Empire, I praise our forbears.*

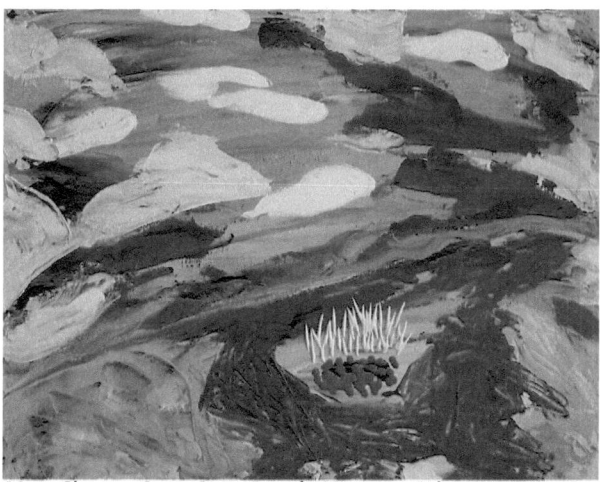

Merry Christmas Santee Sioux! Love the Minnesoata Vikings. 2013.
Acrylic on canvas, 18 x 24"

Review of Spielberg's "Lincoln"

I have not seen the latest big screen hit by Steven Spielberg,
multi-millionaire gatekeeper of the popular American historical
record. But I am sure it is filled to the scalp with good triumphing
over evil, eventually, after evil gets its prime pick of the impoverished hoards.

Abraham Lincoln instigated the murder of 600,000 people. He
and his war party wouldn't just let the unhappy south go. Not because the majority of southern light skins feared out of their minds
their dark skinned slaves (which they most certainly did), and Abe
was going to punish their unchristianity with expensive artillery
and boy meat in order to free their day and nightmares of slave
revolt and retribution—No, honest Abe, like today's puppet presidents, was a political tool of the establishment. He got his orders
from private pressure. For whatever reasons, unknown today like
droning babies in Pakistan will ever be known tomorrow, Abe set
his mind to kill a bunch of politically ignorant farm boys to prove
a point. He and his counterpart Jeff Davis executed about 500 of
their own just to show that state business would always trump the

harvest-or-starvation business of families.

The Emancipation Proclamation (as if an entire race of individuals had to wait for an unwashed, frontier lawyer to declare their freedom), was an inspiration for the masses, a war tactic, and maybe even a private joy for a closet abolitionist President, but it does not negate the reality of Abraham Lincoln as Ghengis Kahn-like slaughterer of innocents.

My ancestors in Hamilton, N.Y. hated slavery, preached abolition, and yet still sewed farm shirts with textiles grown by slave labor. Hypocrites yes, but not deserving to be conscripted to die while a President-king and his wife complained to the cook about too much salt in the sauce. Yet they were, and their friends and brothers died from battle or later from wounds and conditions caused by the war. I still hold the U.S. government accountable for their wrongful deaths. As should any person descended from that "peculiar institution" called the *United States of America*.

Oh yes, and the Santee Sioux have a right to desecrate the memorial to the "Great Emancipator" whenever on holiday in our nation's lockdown capitol. As all American schoolchildren know, he, the great Abraham Lincoln, signed on to the largest mass execution in American history.

And then had some ex-slave cook his dinner.

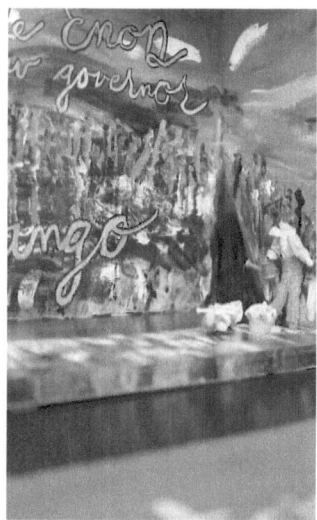

The Past Governor Waterboarding the
Present Governor from *Panem et Circenses*.
2013. Acrylic on old secretary

Look @Nazis!

The failed jock in math class, the high school linebacker that you
feared would take you down in front of *her*, got second string at
the state college and finished his education at the police academy.

Now he is your neighborhood Nazi taking orders from lawyers
and businessman (other failed jocks of the third string). You and
me must hoe our beans with the lawful eye above. The constant
eye. We might not even see it, but it can see *her*. Thank god for
sugar cereal my countrymen. Thank god for car payments and
Rolaids.

Yesterday I got a reply of my installation query from a local
curator. She said I fit on a long line of political art. Which gave the
gentle reminder that, "conscience is for poor people".

Can there be any art apolitical while little drones are spying?
Yes. Hence the World Wars, Vietnam and the gutter slut sorority
chant of "Let's nuke Iraq".

Should not the plumber be banging a pipe with intense retribution? The roofer whizzing shingles at the neck of the banker who foreclosed on *her* dreams? Will the diner waitress ever brave-up to sweeten the crooked cop's coffee with antifreeze? The pretty artists, those brushing above the politics of anti-liberty, the ones sucking up to the androgynous superpower of New York City, which is always wide awake, guilty in bed with the failed jocks, behave like they actually know what the hell is going on in people's hearts and minds. A pretty flower in a meadow, rendered with an O'Keeffe flare, or an abstract in the tradition of "squirt for recognition", is just what the bankers ordered. And then they delivered to your local police force a refrigerator box of steroids and bought up all the drawings Picasso threw under his bed in shame.

"Voila!" A police state with enough artist "intellectuals" to support wholeheartedly the huge power grab of the failed jocks. The historians of art paint word keys to open doors for the young and ambitious. The latter join the upper ranks of professional jealousy or "starve" amidst the "song of the crickets" to their inspired work. The cycle continues unabated while the community works, eats and sleeps, oblivious to the growing, unnatural power of its own paid employees called the local police.

And no artists blow up the bridges.

Time for some drone poem:

Without the help of rabies
Cats cannot kill cats
Soldiers kill a lot of babies
The U.S. says are stats

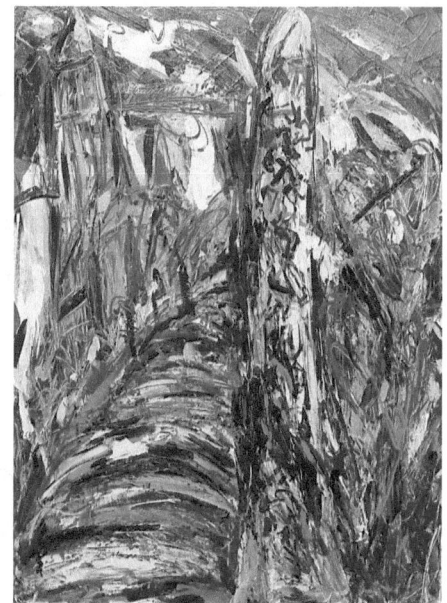

Guns Along the Providence River. 2012.
Acrylic on canvas, 24 x 18"

Seeing Red

I don't know where to begin. I feel that I am losing my sanity in
a topsy-turvy political world. Americans are so sleepy today. Soma
pill overdose perhaps. Senator Rand Paul of Kentucky hosted
a 13 hour filibuster to raise awareness that the U.S. Senate will
confirm a C.I.A. drone-loving psychopath to the position of chief
secret-killer. You can watch the entire speech on the Internet. Mr.
Smith went to Washington to advocate for the boy's club, but all
the boy's club got was a secret drone sent peeping at their Tom's.
Honestly, if Paul is spouting crazy talk then I am Alice down
the rabbit hole, to use the Lewis Carrol comparison he opens
with. Americans impeached a President for spying on his political
counterparts after nine years of rice harvesters getting napalmed
couldn't move an honest senator to scratch his fat ass, for fear of
catching the King's disapproving look. They did it again when a

President lied about an extramarital affair moments after ordering the explosion of babies out of their high chairs in Baghdad. If we don't impeach a President for claiming the authority to murder citizens he dreams are conspirators against his power, then from this day forward I am going all George Grosz on his career. My chastising of America will cease the day a born again Taino culture rises to power.

Senators, I am on to you monsters also. You stinking, colon-rot, corporate stool zombies. If that tool of terror Brennan gets nominated, I vow to immortalize your pre-Nazi filth onto big, big, big canvas.

What have I got to lose? Under the present-day President's duress, only my brains splattered on the highway.

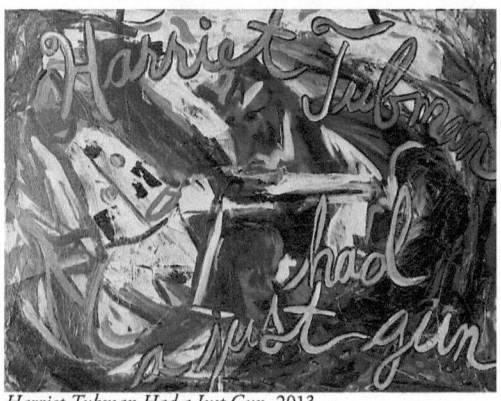

Harriet Tubman Had a Just Gun. 2013.
Acrylic on canvas, 18 x 24"

Harriet Tubman Had a Just Gun

Is there an American man or woman who thinks politics out with reason? I believe that to live without a deep respect for history makes the majority of us both thick-headed and overly polite on contact. Dangerous combination, for it keeps undercovers unresolved issues and allows for democratic thinking (mob conditioning controlled by propaganda) to always get the upper hand.

Harriet Tubman had a just gun. Frederick Douglas bade good

morning to his every day. Bad is not gone because CNN says it's so. Ask the Mayor of New York City to get rid of his private security guards packed to the square jaws with guns and ammo, and he'll go silent with a dumb billionaire smile, and send his goons following you down the street. Otto Frank would have appreciated a gun for dignity. Any Lakota would use his to pick at a rock eye on Mount Rushmore. The mightier power of the state will always get the upper hand on paper. But that has never been the right reason for a people to fall down on their backs like puppies wiggling their limbs to power.

Keep the guns for dignity. If you happen to commit a capital crime with it, count yourself as dignified and distinguished as any President of the United States.

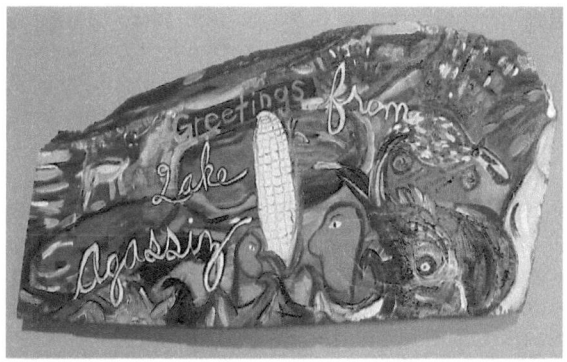

Greetings From Lake Agassiz. 2012. Acrylic on shale, 9 x 16"

Michelangelo the Brown-Noser

It's true. He was a kiss-ass. The greatest renderer of all time. But no artist. Not like the queer Seneca boy with the gift of the seer who carved an ugly French monster in the clay. Some tribal elders nodded their heads. The rest just laughed at his unmanliness. Michelangelo was a pompous servant-user. A Pope's boy. But not an artist. Popes didn't want art, they wouldn't know what to do with it if it slapped their cheese with a brick. Michelangelo was the greatest of the great copiers. His fame is the church. He is iconic because he was the establishment's choice, and all the other great renderers of his time, not quite as technologically sound, were lucky for a nightly loaf of moldy bread. Those wild ones, the intensely expressive of meager talent, the feelers, were lying about in dungeons and dung heaps gibbering away like mad. Today's Michelangelos are a PhD a dozen, and their reward is a $1500.00 mortgage and occasional self-assurance. I imagine the Medici gopher, the Pope's stooge, the man who today is known as the Great Michelangelo, losing sleep in fear that God would not deliver that perfect color in the morning, the one to please his patron, the exact one to insure another gold coin.

So the million dung heap feelers alive today are still dragging their feet over the old earth, carrying an immense chip on their shoulders. Because of the greatest renderer of all time, all painters secretly in their hearts pine to be the success of this man who no doubt in my mind was nothing more than a constipated middle-management aristocratic sissy who would have had his own mother drink the hemlock if the bankers told him to. Michelangelo was the greatest drawer and colorer available to Pope Julius II (Raphael was busy on another astounding commission). And the huge majority of real people on earth at the time were fearing for their lives a God who on a heavenly whim, would wipe away their hard-fought harvest. We know nothing about the people's artists. Nothing because it would have been impossible for them to exist in an economy of "everybody shrink and starve except the golden circle of God's chosen few". Hence dungeons and the dung heap for all expressionists of the 1500's. The Pope would probably have his soldiers run a blade through any peasant who dared attempt a sitting for service at the Sistine.

But the lowly artist did exist, even if no brush ever wiped egg paint on a flat stone.

Today we suffer the legacy of absolutist art. That is all people's first private critique. After that, they wait with their mouths open for the great galleries and museums (more PhD's) to tell them what is worthwhile. Sometimes just money decides, and that brings control back to the absolutist.

Oh well. Back to the basement. At least my bread is not moldy.

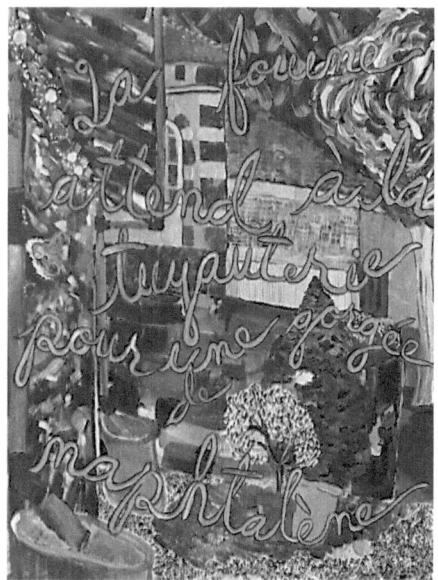

The Stone Marten Waits at the Pipe Fitting for a Sip of Naphthalene. 2012.
Acrylic on hardboard 18 x 14"

France Residency Application: Why Do You Want to Cross an Ocean to Paint?

My answer:

Honor.
The chance to hold my head high. Erica Jong wrote about Henry Miller's enlightenment while living in France. In the New York of 1930 (today still) a writer was a bum if his time was not fraught with appointment and paid schedules. Miller wrote "ecrivain" on his passport, and passed through French customs a healing man. I seek a similar medicine.
Already I have a twenty-five year dedication to writing and painting that has paid absolutely no bills, yet has raised two beautiful daughters along an artistic path. My wife is my sole support.

I would bring to your studio an eager determination to work in my allotted time. Rose (my wife) would receive reward for her husband's bad choice of American career. Meditations about the place would begin to cure a creeping heart sickness that among other nasties, hinders creative effort and sets so many to look upon a downward path of status, rather than forward to joy.

I know my painting is sublime. But I am the only one. France will give the reminder that the rest of the world wants me to paint too.

Presently I am working on a genealogical installation of portraits of eleven generations, movie, published book, and collage entitled "End of the Line," for I am the last Throop in the male lineage, and I feel the need to go out with a happy hum rather than a hopeless whimper. On the back burner awaits attention on a series of paintings aiming to stop the hydrofracking industry from invading our beautiful upstate New York countryside. At your studio I would work on painting(s) to juxtapose your countries' dedication to the beautiful with my people's lust of the fast buck.

We are easygoing, grateful, and gracious people with humor. I have been preaching Giono's joy to the world for a generation. At home it presses up against a bubble we share. Now we blow the bubble to France and make it burst.

Thank you for looking over my work. I hope it is to your liking.

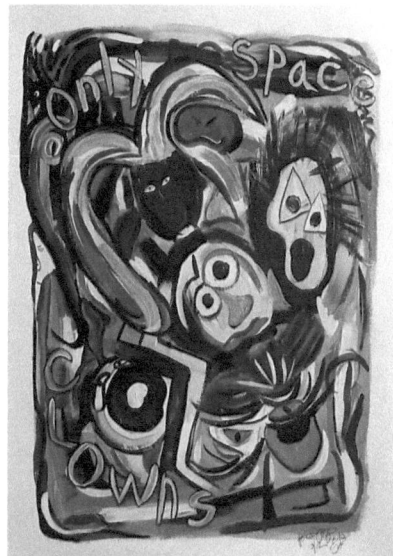

Only Space Clowns. 2012.
Acrylic on paper, 21 × 14"

If There is a Genuine Need It Will Be Met

I have been mourning the passing of paints from my basement floor. For some reason the start of summer has always been my starving time as a painter. House money is tight so I succumb to the urge with cheap craft paint or practically any liquid medium that will stain. Needless to say it is frustrating. No fun at all. Like beating weapons into plowshares, painting good pictures with inferior pigment is a dreamer's dream and will never become a reality in this era.

That is why we must age poetically with friends.

Eric and Dinah have chickens and they supply our family with good eggs. So it was no surprise to me last Friday night to get our ration after their bonfire party. I got the dozen home and into the refrigerator and let them be until breakfast time on Sunday morning.

The butter was hot in the pan, my inside cheeks fleeking saliva,

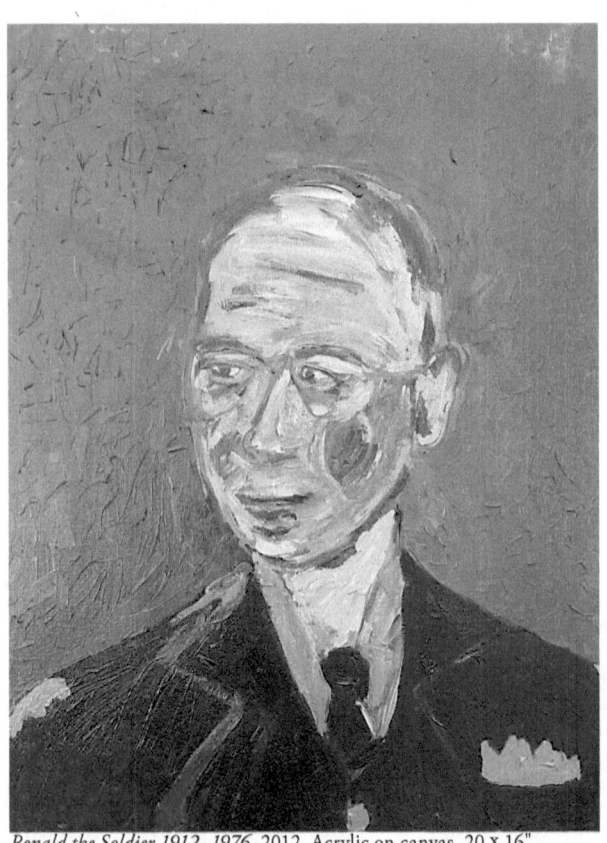

Ronald the Soldier 1912–1976. 2012. Acrylic on canvas, 20 x 16"

and *what?!*

A miracle. Six tubes of expensive Golden Paints discovered inside the egg carton! A need realized. I do not suffer cancer yet, and I can walk with my legs still attached at the hip. Lucky for me my wife has a job that pays for hypertension control... Yet when it comes to paint, I am impoverished. Thank you wise friends. You are one of the couples invited to my shuffleboard future.

Ancestor Worship

Dear County Weeklies,

An old man is reading political propaganda books from the city library. He is thinking over what he read, getting mad, and writing out slapdash vitriol to "folks" in the *Letters to the Editor* section of your free paper. He is going to save the world from the ravages of our socialist President. He thinks natural gas and nuclear power will provide the necessary means to triple his grandson's diabetes-soaked Big Mac intake. Your little shopper with the 10,000 door-to-door mail distribution usually prints either a "Thank you" from a charity event, his mental retardation, or both. Never a counter nor a rebuke to the ignorant government-speak of morons. An opinion is not the problem. Published stupidity is. And this guy takes the cake.

I believe your unwanted shopper's merits lie in its written record of the state of our nation. We have dumbed down this culture to subterranean rock bottom. What should have been born from the union of a fabulously rich people and the glorious invention of antibiotics was a Christmas on earth; a dream that up to a few generations ago was impossible to imagine. A twentieth century of plenty, World Wars to end all war, people marching and suffering for a better tomorrow, never to come. Paradise was born stillbirth. So we settled for day labor and night TV. Empathy a drag. Apathy the new black. Great wealth and safety breeds lethargy. No matter what our philosophical depth, we share the old man's complaint that there aren't enough jobs to support our smart phone habits.

We have forgotten how the milk is obtained and complain about the rising price of milk. That local business (which is representation of its people) invests mucho bucks advertising in your paper is mark of the desperation of our times. Clarity be damned! Let's make a buck.

With this small show of reverence to my forebears (*End of the Line* exhibition) I hope to shed light into the tunnel vision of myself and community.

We need help!

I say look to it in our past. The ancestors are there for everyone. A researched investigation into their trials and tribulations will bring a needful shame upon our houses. The past is not George Washington, any more than it is Mao Zedong or Joe DiMaggio. It is my great-great grandmother. It lies in whatever her before and after says it was. Isn't it obvious? Without her joy, sorrow, desire, fear, and ultimate procreating success, there would be no present. A certainty. Our ancestors shared a mutual respect, a fierce Golden Rule, that never ever crossed the line. Re-learn it. Regard it. Revere it. The vitriolic old man offering up his idiocy to all and sundry is not practicing some individual freedom he ever earned from an oppressive power. That is history conveniently forgotten. He is spreading a disease that we are susceptible to when a community allows an unsubscribed paper to normalize ignorance. Our opinion master is fretting over the President while his grandchildren find joy in head shops and get "art" in tattoo parlors.

Lovely.

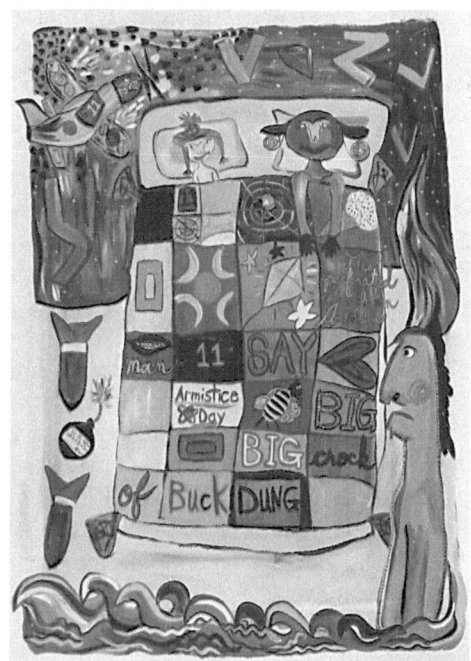

Happy Armistice Day! 2008.
Acrylic on paper, 25 x 16"

Our Unplace in Nature

We do not understand our place in nature. I don't think it can be helped. A raccoon with a human mind would also stomp to death flowers and bugs while searching for neurosis in the Garden of Eden.

Yesterday upon leaving Cooperstown a bit peeved that all that gooey old money ignored my work again, I stopped to visit with some ladies standing in front of the town hall holding signs protesting the wars, drones, and kill lists. I walked up to them bearing one of my paintings, the one where children are nesting for bed under a fat cozy quilt, while U.S. bombs rain down from above, and a perforated American Indian man says "Armistice Day be big crock of buck dung." I set the painting against a tree and asked my fellow sufferers to critique. Of course I thought the message was clear. The bombs were big. The text neat. The children innocent.

One talked about how it reminded her of mural painting in California. The others were mute but smiling, in solidarity of toleration of ten years gathering on Wednesdays to deal with chance crazy people like me. Not one of them "saw" the painting until I explained to them exactly what it was. I then realized a sad personal truth. No one will ever "get" me. To me the painting was visual expression of exactly what they were protesting with signs and chants. Shy Ron got out of the car intent to stand with the choir. Yet I became a preacher by default. After explanation the ladies finally "got" the painting and my politics, and were openly thankful. It wouldn't matter. We turn on our night lights and gas guzzle the life force. The good, the bad, the innocent and guilty, who cares? We all flush our toilets on nature.

I left with yet another example of a prolonged bitter disappointment of mine. When modernly comfortable, the human condition is the only evil in the universe.

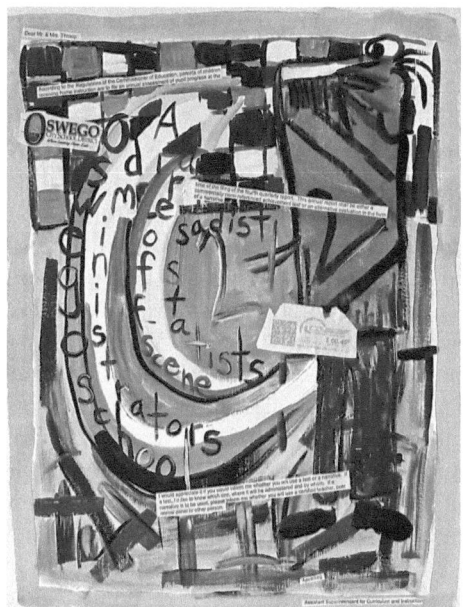

Oswego School Administrators are Off-scene Sadist Statists.
2012. Acrylic on paper, 22 x 15"

In China, Your Knee Caps Get File-Scraped For Homeschooling

Here in the Empire State, the lawyer legislators and cocaine snuffling school boards, are satisfied just to shame the man and woman who naively thought procreation was a private affair.

Plessy vs. Ferguson claimed "separate but equal" crayons colored inside racial lines. Brown vs. Board of Education switched that kind of public idiocy to favor all of humanity, not just the settlers from Northern Europa.

Still, this path to progress occurred at a time when the public school officials thrashed students who had blatant disrespect for elders burdened with the mania of mass babysitting. Also there was a work economy for all to fall into—thousands of white and blue collar positions—all represented and encouraged in America 1955.

Both public school and the economy have since seen dramatic changes.

So what about the right not to go to public school? Who are these local and state fat cats claiming to know my children? We don't want their kind of education. Abraham Lincoln was not a good man. The cafeteria is serving fecal cow on a bun. Most men of science nowadays adhere to personal insanities opposing contentment. My neighbor's kid plays the drums, not calculus. Only a Newton need be a Newton.

I could and should go on. Basically it comes down to the awful reality that anyone can feel discrimination from an oppressive state. It thinks it has the authority to oversee an education that it has no hand in. It reaches deep, hands with fingers fidgeting, counting off the names and numbers of those children not participating in their national squeeze to mass-asphyxiate critical thinking.

With the passage of time many of these homeschooled boys and girls will become the new and improved local leaders of tomorrow. They will remember the second-class citizenship suffered by their parents, the only people, public or private, who educated them under the laws of familial, rather than state, need.

Schools can begin reforming themselves by leaving the hell alone those families who choose different means to positive ends.

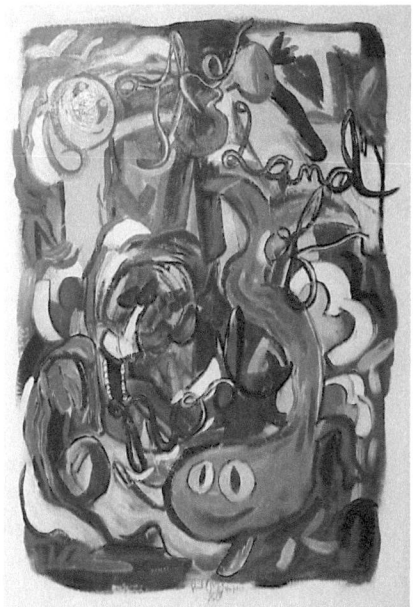

The Land of Nod. 2012.
Acrylic on paper, 23 x 16"

The Joy of Man's Desiring

This is a great book by Jean Giono to remind everyone in the
world that the Industrialized nations have mostly morons for
inhabitants.

Bad morons, not good ones.

Bad morons are those 8–12 year old mentalities who pick their
noses deep, and wipe the yuck under the desk or on their jeans.
They're also the ones who bully and kick, and base a future lifetime around a comfortable income or two.

Good morons are energy, humor, and the Golden Rule. They lead
with enthusiasm, optimism, and a careful show of sensitivity. In
the schoolyard the good moron would be the most just. The bad

moron would be putting a "kick me" sign on the good moron.

Modernity has many good morons, who have exceptional talents to share with the rest of the class in "show and tell." But the bad morons don't care. The bad morons are loud. They laugh in their sleeves knowing darn well that the good morons will be mopping their marble tile in a future "adult" time.

From Mr. Giono, a very good moron:

"...The present time disgusts me, even to describe. It is sufficient merely to endure it. I wanted to make a book with new mountains, a new river, a country, forest, snow, and men all new. The most consoling thing is that I have not had to invent anything at all, not even the people. At this very time when Paris flourishes—and that is nothing to be proud of—there are people in the world who know nothing of the horrible mediocrity into which civilization, philosophers, public speakers and gossips have plunged the human race. Men who are healthy, clean and strong. They live their lives of adventure. They alone know the world's joy and sorrow. And this is as it should be. The others deserve neither the joy nor the sorrow. They know nothing of what they are losing. They think only of adding to their comfort, heedless that one day true men will come up from the river and down from the mountains, more implacable and more bitter than the grass of the apocalypse."

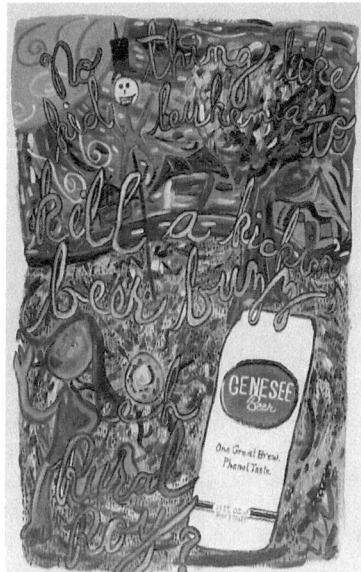

No Thing Like Kid Leukemia to Kill a Kickin'
Beer Buzz, Eh Rural Roy? 2011.
Acrylic on paper, 24 × 15"

Taking Communion

I ride around on a red lawnmower, cutting the grass of acreage
we bought while suffering a winter's funk a few years back. It's
a very beautiful place. One can get to know nature even as an
aggressor, when the flora and fauna all cringe at your arrival, and
those species who can, take off screaming from you.

I dream on the red lawnmower about all the broken stuff in the
human world. Atomization mostly. How it came to be that the
most social animal is now almost completely terrified of being
social. In mid-afternoon I read about mental illness, that half of
all Americans will suffer from some kind of derangement in their
lifetimes. I can read in mid-afternoon, while my daughter plays
her games on the computer, because I have cut myself off from the
modern dementia of "work meticulously alone on meaningless-

ness, and come home ready for dinner". I *am* home. I make dinner, and sweep the floor, and read to my young one. I am home all the time. All the time. Restlessly I can get away once a week to mow acres of meadow and lawn while pretending that I am a philosopher of some note. Really though I am just an invader of saner species doing their own thing without toilet paper. Some sensitive creatures might actually feel the pulse of my thoughts and cringe at the freakishness.

I have an idea for a new book while cutting the grass. A book to finally separate me for good from the rest of my forlorn species. I will scold everyone I know, like and love. Make them hurt, ashamed, admit the truth that they are pathetic, lonely liars. And then in writing I will mock myself sick, content to live as a modern hermit with Lays Potato Chips and a solid month of Texas daylight temperatures above a hundred degrees. To let them know that I know, how they know, that we all know the human system is broken, and yet nobody seeks repair, just maintenance networks of niceties. And then to our coffins.

I get home from my mow and watch a nature movie about the oceans. The narrators all but spell out, "There is evil and its name is 'human'." My pre-pubescent daughter knows the truth, and she erupts, "I hate human beings!" I think to myself what a good title for all books from now on that matter. The many insipid works of *I Hate Human Beings* in a hundred volumes, and then Armageddon.

Marie and I talk on the front porch most mornings before her work bell rings. Today it was about her copier repairman who got into trouble with his supervisor. He went on a call up north to repair a machine for a company named BAXTER that raises beagles and ferrets for military experiments. He asked the woman what that means,

"Do you mean to tell me that you breed these animals to kill them?"

Her face went stone and she called up his supervisor to demand that they send someone else to fix the copiers. She didn't like to be reminded that she was a giant filth-snatch of a human being.

And nobody, not even Marie, told him about the chicken, fish and cow torture he digests through his rotting alimentary canal while farting careful pleasantries day after day after day.

Wrong and right is so blurred, that we're picking off skinny Jews daily in our Schindler's list lives.

We order pizza for the movie and the delivery guy drives up in a Ford Super Duty truck. Gas is $3.82/gallon. I give him a three dollar tip, and both of us tacitly agree to shoot bullets through the heads of Muslim mommies in the Middle East.

And these are my friends, family, and neighborhood characters, outrageous clown monsters like me.

Here lies my joy covered up, circa 2013.

In 1913 I couldn't even dream about the hypocrisy of my neighbor because it never leaked out of the basement. A man might have told a lie or snuck an extra handful of berries when his hungry kids weren't looking. But if he ever got caught, a new town drunk would join the ranks of journeymen horse-shit rakers. There was racism, but it was one way. So it made all the negroes pleasant to look at. They said "Yes sir" to their light-skinned "betters", and there was racial play-mixing of the children as long as mama dark face wiped out the cupboards for mama light face. Now most paranoid light skins swear they can see a circle of black skins on the street giving what's due to a middle-aged light skin and his Birkenstocks. Truthfully though, if any of these smart phone "black" brothers, now totally dependent on the distribution capabilities of their wireless god, lived a day like an Alabama negro, circa 1913, they would immediately chomp back onto their mama's breast sucking out sweet milk. Today, for reasons well documented, a new majority of pure racists are of a much darker complexion. They don't have any lust for pretend revenge. Just blind hatred for non-existent ghosts of the past.

In 1913 there was hypocrisy undercover, and the word "hypocrisy" alone labeled the worse of the worst. The only celebrity who knowingly "loved" his kids was Mark Twain. And look what that got him... A bunch of dead kids. He stayed in hotels conversing with beautiful women. He snacked off plates of danishes in drawing rooms. He made morality a profession and lectured about a conscience to people too burdened with the beginnings of a deranged one to notice that they were being played by the grandest of charlatans. And just think of all the negroes getting lynched or ignited in the surrounding counties on Saturday night. Today the celebrities can possess practically the opposite of a conscience. Or one that gobbles up its narcissistic host like a very sexy corporate whore. According to our God the Media, after 500 years of immense social suffering, the American negro has aspired to the celebrity goodness of a millionaire Beyoncé. Or an NFL millionaire scum bag thumping crying dogs with a stick. Or a millionaire President who wipes up other brown oppressed peoples over the globe with a bloody rag. And the dark-skinned kids still won't play with the light-skins. Long ago, the beginnings of big government insured the enslavement of a people in autumn, and the following spring gave up that responsibility entirely. In 1913 all people, dark and light, were kept very busy before a big god that still held sway in the broad and terrible heavens. Now even the evangelicals of Evanston watch out for the man-made space junk raining from the skies. They look up from time to time while speaking through their wireless gods.

Black and white. The god damned overfed idiots of America!

In 2013, 64 negroes aren't tied to a incendiary global cross. All earthlings are.

Jerry the talking handyman is definitely not a racist. Oh boy does he look the part though. He is cordial, although it's easy to see that he hates like a racist. He is quick to judge. He is openly reactionary. If you're not careful, he will hate you very quickly. Not being careful means disagreeing with him. He likes to talk politics, and his politics lean left, which means he wants to entrust the morality of earth to a huge bureaucracy with light-skinned billionaires at the helm. So, evil Kraft, Inc., with its empire of mustard and mayonnaise is allowed to exist as long as all people, light and dark and in-between, are free to tongue-wash their gums with Kraft products *and* go to college.

Jerry considers himself a liberal-independent. He wants the world to have a Coke and entitle his people, which is all the people, total control over a '99 Ford Ranger pick-up. Very similar to Fidel Castro's dream without the bummer of a blockade. Jerry refuses to see that if seven billion people all have rights to the same resources Jerry worships, then our planet will wake up with a start and swat its parasitic fleas.

Yet I believe sincerely that Jerry is the smartest that any of us will ever be. He just doesn't have any sense. A chicken steaming in every pot on the same day, from Addis-Ababa to Albuquerque would result in a mass, wasting suffering of all the earth's human children, and a whole helluva lot of disenfranchised chickens.

No, Jerry. You, me, all the beige and brown unknowns of Ethiopia and pallid 43° and up latitudinals, are non-useful idiots. All our lives we partake in the generational torture of our own God(s), to throw our faith in some nineteenth century, unwashed English youth who took a five year-long voyage around the globe, yet could only come up with a theory that has made us all suicidal in our sleep. A man, who while on board, and even in a room off the kitchen at home, wiped his ass with a bare hand and left the lingering shit-smell on for dinner. I would give up my God and yours too, if because of this deep-thinking, visionary wonder, thousands of species weren't kicking the evolutionary bucket before their time. But just the opposite is true. Because of Chuck Darwin, Jerry drives a red pick-up, and upright American Presidents slaughter babies in their cribs. All present-day gods and god-affiliates cruise *Beagles* around the earth, trawling the sea floor to wipe out another one of their beloved creatures. They recruit entitled morons like Jerry and me to wrench out some painful gush of moral diarrhea.

Impossible. Impossible. Impossible to articulate to the masses with Kraft mayonnaise available for sale. Do you see?

The earth spins to provide for Jerry a personal cache of toiletries. Mommy and Daddy loved him so much that they made him emperor of a universe where his across-town friend and the old lady next door think that they are emperors too. Jerry is right about evil big business. It has usurped our souls. Yet neither he nor I will sharpen a knife to stick through the belly of policy-makers and their product police protecting habits and habitats leading to mass extinction.

What this means is this: Jerry is a good, non-Jew German, circa 1937.

Do I want to get closer to my fellow man? Or do I want him to just leave me the hell alone until I request his use as a human mirror? Hell is other people. Even the most non-intrusive friendly can be a real pain in the soul. I do three things that occupy my time. Homemaker, husband and homeschooler. The homemaker covers a lot of ground. That is all chores of drudgery and love. I am father and cook, window-washer, stair-wiper, laundry man, waker-upper, tucker-inner, and cat litter-scraper. The husband is everything the homemaker is, plus eighty percent thoughtful, compassionate, and considerate. I don't ever ask for new underwear until standing before her, wearing the old, trumps all previous "good" acts of a man. The last time I purchased a shirt for myself was on our anniversary, 2004. I am the hair-shirt husband, and appear to be thriving at the position. A closer look would discover the modern-day lunatic hand-slapping his genitals with a cross expression.

The homeschooler is teacher and role model. That is eight subjects covered in-depth for the undeclared fascists on the school board, plus near total mind, body, and soul care of another human being.

My free time is an hour some nights spent painting with acrylics.

I have many paintings. Some are framed. Few sell, because in my heart I know that the European business model is insane. At night I go down into the basement to paint, like I write, what I feel is right.

Tim stops by with Jane to visit. They bring cherries. Tim is an adjunct professor at the community college. He got a gig judging the art work for a show put on by the local art association. His pick for Best in Show was a pencil drawing copy of a photo of John Lennon by a fourteen year old girl. Many artists of Oswego County applied. Fortunately for Tim's and my burgeoning relationship I did not. Tim is an art history teacher. That is, you can read about the artist's visual sufferings in expensive books. Fascinating anecdotal lives of the artists. Paul Klee can be drawing pictures at the kitchen table getting scolded by his wife who is a dunce. He renders like an armless seven-year old, and colors just how anyone would imagine a Swiss grown-up would color. Neat. No mess. Between the lines. Balanced bank book. Deep thinker. Tim has his Dunkin' Donuts scholars read up on Klee, after supper, after Pizza Hut, after Ipod and smartphone, after American Idol, K-mart no. 2 pencils, and a whole aisle of Chinese factory-supplied Target wall hangings, one of which is a copy of a photo of John Lennon in the autumn of 1972. The little fourteen year old brat knows who he is. Daw! He's on Youtube. Her doppleganger Justin Bieber boyfriend wears sunglasses just like that. They're called "John Lennon glasses".

Perhaps Tim is representative of the second-tier of art aficionados of America. "The Renderists". If you can copy like a very patient monkey, then you are an artist of the county and worthy of wide-spectrum admiration. If the subject matter is "cool", like a photograph of John Lennon, or Eartha Kitt, or Elizabeth Cotton, or even just the curving vagina of a look-alike anybody, then your chances at local art success are very good. The third tier deals mainly in tattoos and motorcycle gas tank art, also needing a render reality, so the mind won't ever slip away into sensitive dream. The third tier secretly aspires to the second tier where status is granted by the established keepers such as Tim. Inky ass drawings pay, but pride is the top prize at the photo-copied county art contest.

The first tier is the corporate conspiracy of art. The collectors. Take a photograph of a naked nine-year old standing in a junk yard, with the word "turd" drawn onto her belly in lipstick. Title it "My Mother's Candle," and seduce a popular New York gallery owner, if you're an attractive man, and he's a man. Same for an attractive woman, yet don't expect to get very far, because its always been and always will be a man tier. If you're a woman who looks like a man, or talks like one, or can spread the fear of an angry god through the child population like one, then you'll O'Keeffe the tier just enough to faux-balance it and perpetuate the teaching of the first tier unto the second. Hence Tim preaching the fine art gospel of millionaires getting taught by wealthy gallery-owners what constitutes art, and the business of art. What to invest in. How to get richer.

The child turd photograph sold for seven hundred thousand at Christies' September auction. The fourteen year old John Lennon copier got a hundred bucks and a write-up in the local shopper. Tit Painter Tattoo Terry gets fifty bucks an hour to draw a dragon on a hot crotch. The true artist is any he or she who would blow up the bridge of this phony "live and let live" philosophy that connects our myriad trash can paths of insanity leading to mass extinction.

Not communing very well, am I?

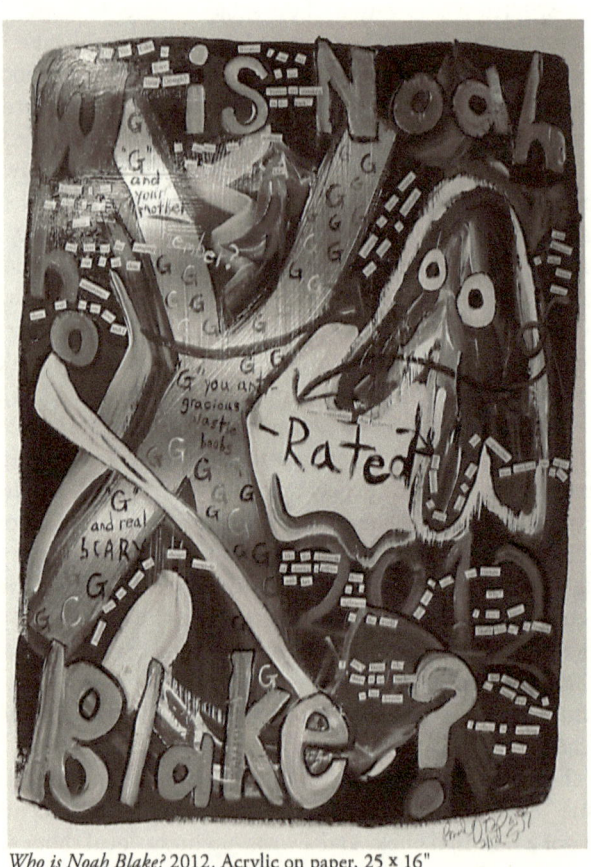

Who is Noah Blake? 2012. Acrylic on paper, 25 × 16"

Who is Noah Blake?

Well, the antithesis of greed of course!

The protaganist of a fictional journal depicting the life of an American boy in 1801.

But *Adbusters* Magazine cannot relate to an early 19th century paradigm, even if it came with antibiotics and virus inhibitors.

What modern-day, urban Canadian hopes someday to ride on a sleigh with a hot potato in his lap?

I have received their Starbuck's rabble rousing periodical for a year. Midway through I realized that, like all cultured and voiced North Americans, the Vancouver editors were helpless idiots too, no different than their colleagues at *People* magazine, or the even more myopic *New York Times*.

It is still propaganda, but worse, much worse with its repeating strikes to spark the innocent and vulnerable into messy action.

It's a loud west coast rainy whine, with fifty thousand distribution channels to fashionable doom.

Adbusters, like the phony capitalists it pretends to abhor, is the problem. It says there is the boogeyman uncontrollable greed inside everyone of us.

Really? I do not know anybody whose #1 hobby is acquisition. Not a one. If I knew the editor of *Adbusters* I might count an actual acquaintanceship with a greedy troll of the human race. For they do exist, albeit in very low numbers.

No, everyone I know is thinking simple love dreams on Valentine's Day. Even the sheet-rocker and his daughter at the register purchasing a box of Betty Crocker brownie mix. He might be the most uncreative sloth of Anytown, America, but will probably adjust much quicker in an economic or ecological crisis. That hot potato will come in handy for family survival on a cold, unelectrical night. On the other hand, judging from the graphic corporate dependency of *Adbusters*, a well-timed brown out or two would drive these charlatans to an end of days rife with desperation and pillage.

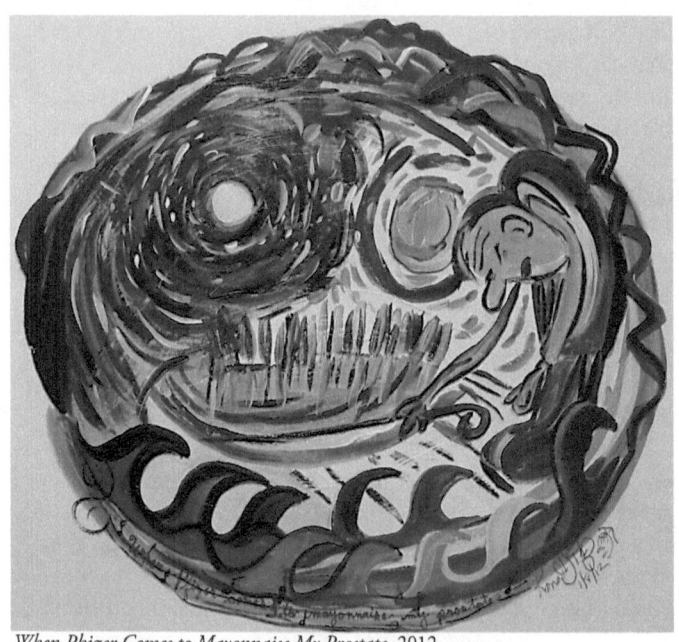

When Phizer Comes to Mayonnaise My Prostate. 2012.
Acrylic on paper, 12 x 12"

When Pfizer Comes to Mayonnaise my Prostate

Here is another health care painting. A friend brought some small frames over, and I will honor his kindness with more work that will inspire a revolution in free thinking.

Maybe that old man in the painting is me picking carrots before my morning stretches. First the sun and then the moon, and long naps in the
afternoon.

I'll have to get south if I want a greased prostate. A regimen of exercise, small portions of grass-fed meat, and an inordinate amount of carrots with ginger might issue forth a new old age where Dr. Polyp can display his colonoscope in the curio cabinet.

Who knows?

God forbid my heart physician ever read a book on nutrition. Twenty-five years ago he and his medical army thought that ingesting squeezed fish juice for circulatory health was wacky quack medicine. Fifty years ago he allowed his own kids to be grabbed out of gestation with salad tongs. My own great-great grandfather walked down a line at Gettysburg sawing off limbs with who knows what fecal grease smeared on his finger nails.

Never get me wrong. The accumulated knowledge from time and practice have made our species the best life-savers in history. But it is still just practice. Certainly doctors the world over would prefer being better life preservers and sickness preventers?

After five visits in over a year, this basement painter with hypertension could subsist on a diet of human hair and gasoline, and exercise like a drunken sloth on a hot day, yet still not get asked the most important question by the doctor and his team. "What are your ingestion habits Mr. T.?"

Oh well. Looks like you'll have to heal thyself, broken painter.

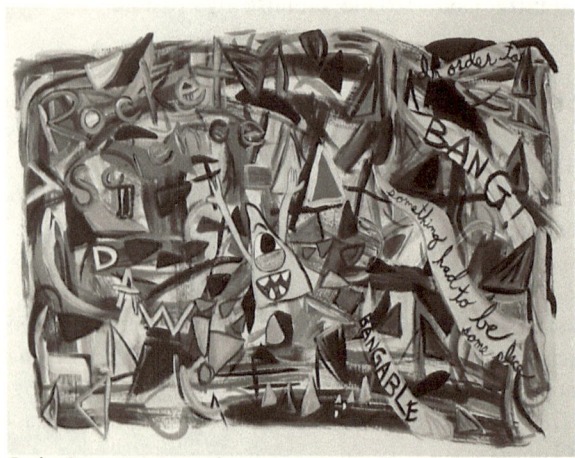

Rocket Science! 2011. Acrylic on paper, 15 x 22"

In Order to Bang!

Is there a physicist, astronomer, cosmically enlightened trout angler who would explain to me the big bang? I have felt its onto-logical pressure push on my skull cap for twenty years now, and still no scientist can or will unveil the scene of pre-fourteen billion years ago. The big boom had to pow-wow from something, yes? If the universe today was once the size of an unmovable pinhead, then where did the big nothing hide the pin? Or, for that matter, the pin cushion, sewing table, foot pedal, floor, ceiling, roof, and sky?

So are we a universe in universes?

Any one hungry care?

Here is another six million dollar painting to trade in for a mega-grant to satiate the twaddle of highly educated infant dreamers. Never feed the lowly Somalians. Feed the Poindexter's of astronomy, hundreds and thousands of them, leaping into the safe, lawful arms of Hubble and Newton, more for a clingmanship to earthly careerism than any faith in a human-made scientific method. Mock the people's Gods. Mock the human weaknesses. So easy to do when guaranteed a gob of money.

See? We must be right about the nothing. Look at all the humanity wealth falling from the sky as divine space junk!

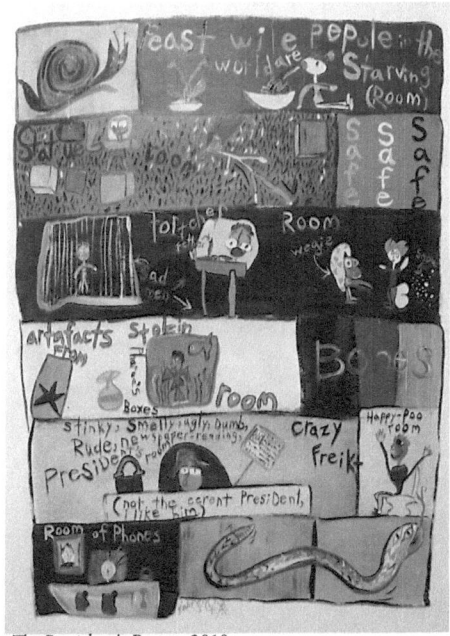

The President's Rooms. 2010.
Acrylic on paper, 23 x 16"

The President's Rooms

These are the rooms visitors aren't allowed in. Check out that wedgie.

I think that Americans love to plug the auspices of their luxury prisons on holiday. They haven't much else to be politically proud of. I actually know a kid who works for the U.S. military in eastern Cuba washing dishes, clothes, and teeth of the kidnapped guests all suffering the highlights of the same repeating nightmare. God only knows what other humiliating acts the private is performing for a paycheck and a yellow ribbon 'round the stock-art oak tree Google has displayed today.

Research Armistice Day, along with the Kansas super-jingo congressman, and the Generalisimo President who reversed its memorial nobility. Then maybe we can all come to the understanding that just touching a no-bid automatic weapon manufactured by the greatest subsidized industry the world has ever known, and marching with it like a trained monkey, does not necessarily initiate one an honored citizen of the populace.

Today I will congratulate those veterans who resisted a foreign invasion with failed éclat. To my band of brothers circa 1813. We really gave those Brits what's coming, hey boys?

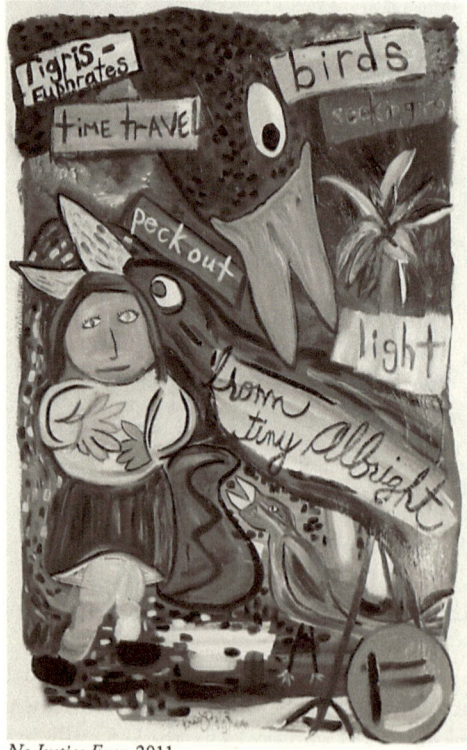

No Justice Ever. 2011.
Acrylic on paper, 23 X 14"

Personals from Sunday Times in Pretend Hell

Political Psychopaths will be encouraged to eat the arms and legs off each other during their eternity in the pretend hell which everyone knows by now—everyone—even the pretend Christians, does not prevent determined priests from lobbing their love eyes at attractive altar boys.

Here is a practical bullet plan for the helpless American to fulfill his or her moral obligation to temporarily relieve animal (which includes human) suffering:

- stay very poor
- have one or two babies with a confident woman
- collect EIC from the masters of war
- buy food and shelter
- enjoy living to the fullest while you wait for their guns and ammo

What could have possibly been Madeleine Albright's incentive to initiate the slow death of 500,000 Iraqi children?

A clean hotel room?

Pleasing a deceased father who ignored her in life because she had girl cells?

One can spend a lifetime career asking for new answers to the already known but unspoken ones. She was a born vicarious killer, self-taught after college and avarice ladder climbing. There are no gray lines on the truth meter. I only wish there was a real hell we could depend on to deliver eternal agony to the death wielders.

But woe. There is no justice ever.

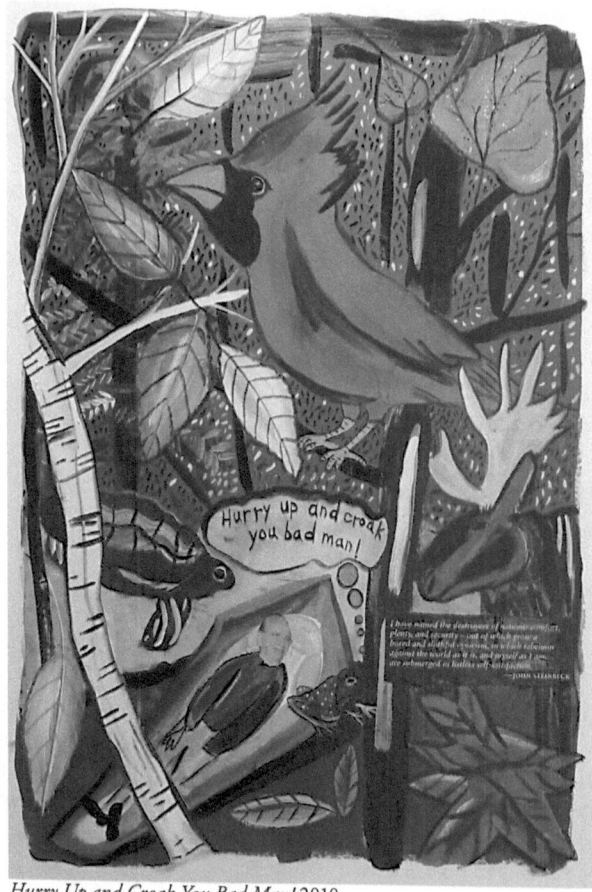

Hurry Up and Croak You Bad Man! 2010.
Acrylic on birch, 22 x 13"

Will Somebody Push Him in Front of a Highway Truck?

Ah yes, the propagandist. The altruistic, the good, the sincere and kind. Can one of us monkeys drop a banana peel on the path of his Hitler strut? Can we skin a whole banana bunch and toss them onto the floor for the corporate dancers to wallop their own faces flat?

This is art. All else is counterfeit during the coming Younger Dryas. The people will eventually get the message, and react. The wrinkly old psycho-snake Murdoch will have no choice but to slither toward his grave, and stop along the way for a Kevorkian shot of what should have been his fate sixty years ago.

How much more sickness spread shall humanity allow before it wakes up to give him the dose he deserves? What is our philosophy? Live and let live? So he has equal right, even by accomplice to thousands of hate crimes, to exist beside your miraculous, pre-pubescent sons and daughters?

The cardinal, turtle, moose and frog would laugh a hearty fat laugh all over your specie-centric ways, if they could fathom just an infinitesimal shred of human hypocrisy. When one of theirs runs amok onto the dark side, and hoards gobs of misery and woe to pulverize the simple joys of nuts and berries, the elders push that rot onto the busy highway and watch for the predator Toyota to crush, or in the case of the moose, dent it to death.

Society on a mass scale has failed. These Murdochs are subtle Nazis. There are about a thousand of them, more or less. And we are seven billion, severely weakened by illusion. Our collective bad breath could waft them back to the hell where they were bred. If only. If only…

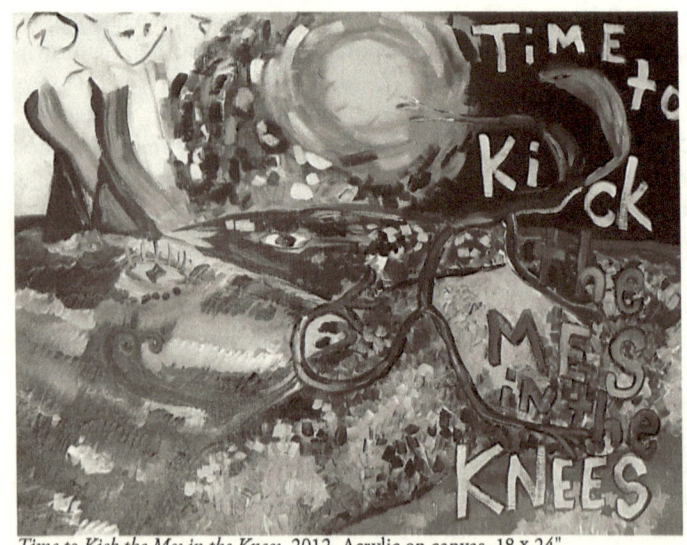

Time to Kick the Mes in the Knees. 2012. Acrylic on canvas, 18 x 24"

Time to Kick the Mes in the Knees

Recently on National Propaganda Radio I heard that one of the 23 MacArthur Foundation Genius Grants (a $500,000.00 prize) went to Junot Díaz, a fiction writer/college professor at MIT. The bio on the foundation website states that he uses "vernacular dialogue and spare, unsentimental prose to draw readers into the various and distinct worlds that immigrants must straddle". He got a phone call out of the blue telling him of his amazing good fortune. According to MacArthur, this stupendously generous grant is unique in that there will be "no strings attached" to Junot's moolah gift, which will be distributed in periodic payments over the next five years.

Kudos to Junot and the Mac people for seeking out easy genius and rewarding it with gobs of money. Pencils are cheap but time is priceless. So I wonder how, in this overflowing economy of staggering wealth poorly distributed... I wonder how our grant hero will make this time award bear genius fruit.

I call it a time reward because Junot is already making about a hundred grand a year teaching creative writing full-time at MIT. Obviously in order to make the best use of the money which buys time, Junot would have to take a five year long hiatus from grading papers and lecturing about creativity to the next generation of geniuses of the establishment. Otherwise he will have to expend all of his future potential devising a time machine or new drug to severely limit sleep without side-effect. This might bring future grant money in the field of physics or biology, but would detract from the initial intent of the award. Junot cannot possibly keep his day job if he is to write more outstanding "unsentimental prose". But I bet he will. After all, he didn't ask for the money. It just came to him. Like it does to all hard-working creative types, who have professorships, and car payments, and wild nights of striped bass entrees in Harvard Square.

This from Henry Miller, a writer of another kind of genius:

"We write, knowing we are licked before we start. Every day we beg for fresh torment. The more we itch and scratch the better we feel. And when our readers also begin to itch and scratch we feel sublime. Let no one die of inanition! The airs must ever swarm with arrows of thought delivered by les hommes de lettres. Letters, mind you. How well put! Letters strung together with invisible wires charged with imponderable magnetic currents. All this travail forced upon a brain that was intended to work like a charm, to work without working. Is it a person coming towards you or a mind? A mind divided into books, pages, sentences replete with commas, periods, semi-colons, dashes and asterisks. One author receives a prize or seat in the Academy for his efforts, another a worm-eaten bone. The names of some are lent to streets and boulevards, of others to gallows and alms houses. And when all these "creations" have been finally read and digested men will still be buggering one another. No author, not even the greatest, has been able to get around that hard, cold fact."

This year Junot got his seat in the Academy. Me, and a million of my contemporaries, are pulling worms out of bones.

It is no wonder I heard about Junot Diaz on NPR. The MacArthur Foundation is a regular contributor to my government radio station. The circle is complete. The Mac people scratch the NPR backs and the favors are always repaid. First advertise, and then via radio vignette proselytize the foundation's normalcy to millions of Americans. Set the standard for what is acceptable genius. In this case, Junot the well-paid writer of immigrants. Good thing he wasn't just some tomato picker in Florida writing out snippets of pure genius among a chorus of snoring co-workers in government barracks. Junot picked fruit all day for a pittance to send back to Mama Flora in La Vega. He always wanted to be a writer. Unlike all the other boys, he loathed soccer and baseball. His grade school teacher thought his big words should never be used by a poor Dominican, yet she tolerated Junot for his humility. By the time he was thirty-five Junot had written over a million words, and thought his depictions of immigrant woe and wonder quite good. He felt the sting of his social class comrades daily. They didn't have time to care, yet tolerated Junot for his shared humility. It helped that he picked tomatoes as quick as the best. His brother Rodrigo, who loved Junot like a saint, got wind of the

MacArthur Foundation on NPR (his American culture station), and promptly sent a post out to Chicago espousing the writing talent of his older brother. Rodrigo made a point to note the adversity Junot faced every day, and how he burned the midnight oil perfecting his craft within an environment that would crush the hopes and dreams of lessor spirits. He sent in one of Junot's short stories and promptly forgot about his good deed amidst a bad dream world of endless tomatoes.

The Mac people received Rodrigo's nomination of his brother and promptly threw it in the trash.

What multi-million dollar organization would risk its resources and reputation on an actual genius migrant worker? The MacArthur Foundation won't drop a nickel searching for aspiring artists who might need more than anything a modest economic and confidence boost. It's got its bases covered. Keep the unlucky hoard picking the nation's fruits and vegetables. Dole out millions to upper middle class safety people, the well-groomed and super careful of our culture. Just review for yourself the 20 or so recipients of any year. This year (2012), besides some mandolin virtuoso, all have established, non-broom-handling jobs or professorships in universities. Not one is hungry or late with the rent. Not one is actually taking any risk with his or her genius. All bases are covered. The MacArthur Foundation people pick winners who are most like themselves. The comfortable car payment types. The Internet connection ones. The college fund for their children folks. The antithesis of needy genius.

I admit there is a bunch of sour grapes in my review of this year's sue-pare geniuses. But I persist to shed light on the power money has when it mixes with Big Media. Impressed upon my mind and a hundred thousand other local listeners of our public radio station is the story of Junot and his receiving a gift of a half million dollars. Attached to that marvelous money prize is the word "genius". Both the NPR and Mac People refrain from actually defining the word, nor provide a disclaimer about their bastardization of it. Junot and the rest of this year's recipients are probably very creative and intelligent people. So yes, by definition Junot is a genius. He wrote some books. That is very creative. The problem with rewarding Junot such an enormous sum of money under the auspice of "genius" is that we (with the push of the propagandists) have lowered the bar for "genius" to mean any full-time university employee who part-times in creativity.

The whole grant procedure mocks the Emerson or Edison among us who never applied for the private safety net, who kept at their genius no matter what Lexus put out that year. And these men and women of old produced movements and machines that will last for centuries. An Elisabeth Cady Stanton, Henry Thoreau, or any Jane or John Doe of our day, one among the unsung thousands who struggle creatively, never make it to the committee round table. The Mac Foundation claims that it "supports creative people and effective institutions committed to building a more just, verdant, and peaceful world". And no offense Junot, but you're the best of the best? You are the creative spokesperson for disillusioned immigrants? Jesus, there has got to be a single mom in Laredo with as much creative drive as you. A writer-to-be who practically crawls into the trailer at night, feeds her babies, tucks them in for poverty dreams, and then sits down to write out her daily agonies creatively. She is someone who would actually take that huge half a million dollar chip on her shoulder and produce at top speed tenfold of what time forbids you to do as status-shopper in the corporate (university) mall.

Allow me to break down an imaginary day typical for a Junot, or any insta-rich hobbyist fiction writer whose day-job is university professor.

MIT is located in a busy metropolitan center. So any commute must be hell. An hour at least from house to office. If you're a married man with kids, then the family will need that part of you allotted to them. That takes morning and evening time away from fiction writing. On your desk await a pile of papers to read and make written suggestions. This is part of your contract. Unavoid-able. The rich brats are paying for your tutelage, so you can't just delegate advice from the grad assistant. Office hours are today and Thursday, and there's a night class on Wednesday. The family is hosting the grandparents next weekend, and it's your turn to cook dinner tonight. Phew. After dinner, if the kids are entertained and the wife is caught up with her own homework, then you'll steal away an hour or two to work on the novel. It's got to be a good one. Your reputation is counting on it. Good thing the creative juices are overflowing. The wife in pajamas waits expectantly for you. Your becoming a Mac-fellow has improved her outlook significantly. You dot the t's and cross the i's, and fall hard asleep, content with comfort.

Genius.

And culture! Poor Junot must also squeeze in television, groceries, sump pump, parties, school plays, cub scouts, swimming pool, tennis, magazines, doctor, cat litter, lawn care, wine cellar. A hundred grand per year for the next five years only exacerbates the problems of modern living. He was perfectly happy with the Volkswagen Passat. Now to think about leasing an upgrade. And the public school in Braintree was fine until junior said the "F" word at karate. Now with the half a million, private Thayer Academy deserves a walk-through.

Surely avarice comes into play. Not a fierce greed, but the gentler kind, where each rung on the incredibly safe corporate ladder improves materially with height. All professions offer the golden rung to its most ambitious climbers. Always a very scheduled and boring climb for the determined. By resume Junot has paid his corporate dues, faithfully and on time. He had reached the silver rung, and now this giant boost from the Foundation has cast him a golden throne on the summit of One-Upmanship Mountain.

None of this reward goes to Junot, the qualified teacher of writing. Supposedly the actual day job that helped push him (and many others) to these new, fantastic heights of national recognition is of no concern to the Foundation. It doesn't matter that Junot might be an incredible bore in the eyes of his students. Or that many of them will finish his class more institutional-like than creative in their writing styles. Or worse—write more like Junot. Fiction-writing neophytes should know who their audience is, and if Junot is the only audience, and Junot is human, he will probably lead his students toward his personal likes and dislikes.

So much for creative writing.

I'd like to know what teaching credentials he has. Junot is a genius, highly intelligent and creative, but does he inspire his students? Is his main focus on their personal development as writers and artists? Is it not an educational conflict of interest to set up a successful commercial writer to teach his future competitors? The grant from the MacArthur Foundation by definition seeks to support Junot in personal creative endeavor, which was born precisely not via the art of teaching, but rather by his one-man writing show. The spark that the Foundation sees in Junot the individual, not dedicated teacher, is what got him the half a million. So will he do the right thing and quit his job tomorrow? Will MIT rethink its policy of placing successful business people into teaching positions, and seek rather those who are born and practiced teachers? Probably no, and no. Junot is an advertisement for MIT. Both MacArthur and the University get their credential boosts from the existence of an "unsentimental writer of immigrants". He might teach like a slow-talking rock, but he's a gem to the charlatans who charge 65 grand a year for impressionable youth to court slow-talking rocks. And the MacArthur people, while stepping on no toes, place another chiseled rock, a perfect fit to its glorious foundation.

Poor Junot. It's not his fault. Our culture is to blame. We are rewarding hyper-atomized professions undeserved wealth and status. For an economy to remain strong, health and wellness are imperative, and by successful implementation will bear modest sustaining fruit. A creative writer is a boon to the community when his or her efforts improve the outlook of children, or reinforce the golden rule to remind brethren not to stray. Junot uses his creative gift toward self-promotion. He is a prostitute of his own mind and its overloaded output. The book has a price tag. It takes from the community. Sure it maintains professions in the design and distribution houses of New York and Singapore, and those jobs generate wealth in other industrialized economies, but the whole effort rewarding Junot perpetuates the bad idea that the world needs more "mes" on an international level. And that means a lot of over-the-top individual solicitation among thousands in similar fields of human endeavor. The long life of the individual is shrouded in too much fruitless effort. Struggle, even after achieving the top evolutionary success of health and wellness, becomes the norm. Everyone still pretending success locks onto the ladder and starts climbing. It's not until after the third prostate exam or mammogram, that dreams of a spiritual kind push their way into the brain. By then the grandchildren arrive and although paths to enlightenment are ready for your commitment, one life in just one lifetime cannot reform the chaotic social disorder all by its lonesome. Vicariously we lock back onto the ladder, and praise the Junots of the world, hoping someday our posterity can reach such equally vaulted heights.

What specialties improve a human race? Very hard to say. Good medicine and smart agriculture, via several generations of careful research and implementation, has brought long life to many. Science has its dark side in nuclear weapons and British Petroleum, yet the balance is kept steady with rapid reduction of infant mortality. More scientists live to count the extinctions. The modern wheel of life has fallen off a monster mountaintop removal truck and wherever the earth shows scars of suffering, humanity has made tremendous leaps and bounds. Both Junot and I are guilty of ocean fish depletion, iceless polar bears, and childhood diabetes. But unlike Junot, I am not a garbage hole. I am an unfunded teeny-tiny kink in the human machine. My creative effort is spent "kicking the mes in the knees". For all of his recognized creative potential, Junot will write more tales about Emperor Man for the "mes" to admire. They'll dole out the 500 grand, not for Junot to unleash his ability to shame us and save the world, but to keep him comfortably quiet amassing status as award-winning writer of all that keeps man a great distance from man.

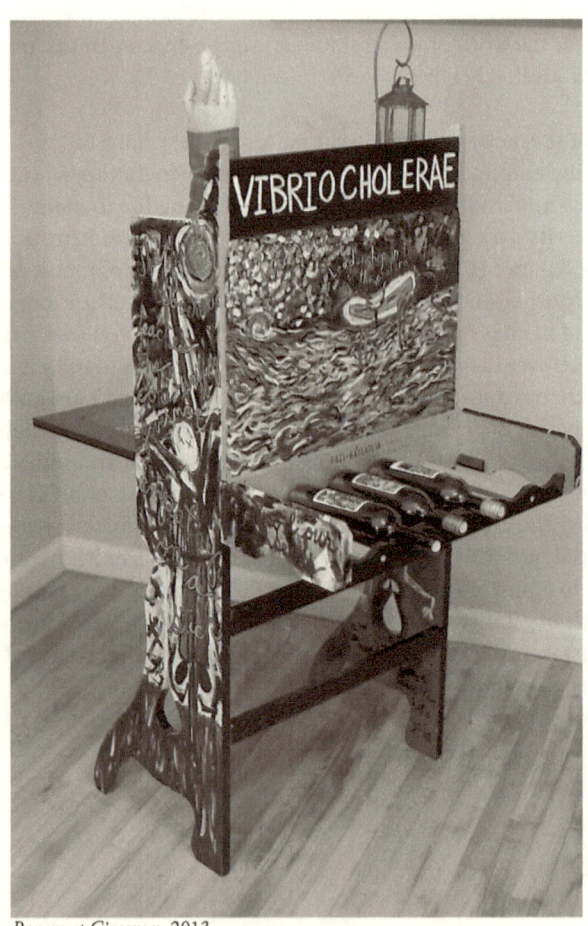

Panem et Circenses. 2013.
Acrylic on old secretary with other stuff, 60 x 24 x 20"

Must Stop the Lower Order of Humanity

I need to get lots of these nature paintings finished before the final assault on the flora and fauna of Central New York. If you live in New York, Syracuse, Rochester, Albany, Buffalo, Binghamton or Utica cities, if you squat on a small backyard, or public park and have factory beef and chicken barbecues and raise babies where the urban veil often blinds you to the natural truth of things, yet still feel that pesky on-and-off pulse of sentiment for life outside of your bubble metropolita, please consider offering a fleeting several seconds of your busy day to the collective mind torture of the men who want to sell you natural gas.

Let's mark a time. Say 3:24 p.m.?

Maybe strong dream justice is all we ever needed to achieve miracles.

Here we are at an infinitesimal point in earth's infinity cycle when mind justice may be our only hope beyond the terror of some real bad collective practices warping out of control.

I am so tired of feeling tired and powerless. Let's sleep on this together.

And dream!

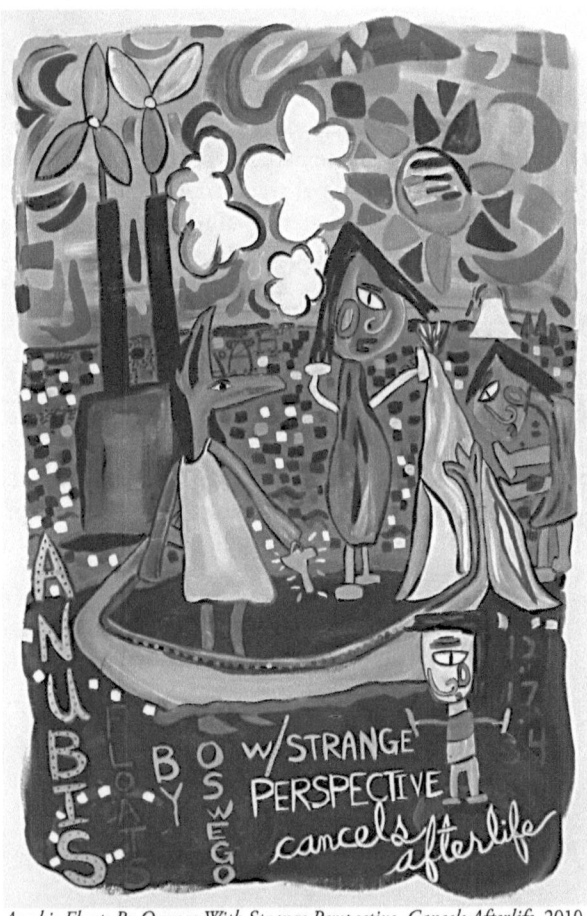

Anubis Floats By Oswego With Strange Perspective. Cancels Afterlife. 2010.
Acrylic on paper, 25 x 16"

Global Warming

Headlines from NPR would have us assume that global warming just stopped, and that summer's upstart is warm breeze and straw-berries and wild fauna nesting soundly in the tall grass, swimming peacefully in pure and wild, wet waters, nibbling moist berries off the endless lush produce of mother earth...

NPR is government propaganda. Someone at the top of their machine is having lunch with Goebbels.

We could stop to get our bearings, reassess our dependencies, head into the future with strong backs and determination, but will not move a millimeter until our dollar takes its final nose dive into oblivion.

Still, with minimal effort we can break out of surface denial by making atmosphere talk our first attempt at every conversation. We could become mindful once again and use our cleanliness and good health and swell science to imitate 14th century Japanese royalty. We could write poetry, take day walks, stab to death the Carnegie Steel and Rockefeller Oil Earth-hating drive-about we depend on more than our neighbors and families. We could nat-uralize our lives with creative job creation. That means we choose our local economies and dress them to our own survival tastes. Oil execs might have to be tortured gently. Fracking giants could have their heads politely lopped off. Military brass would get the picture after a sound fragging by its own sentient cannon fodder.

These punishing days will come. What's unbelievable is that the majority of intelligent human beings refuse to articulate this with any regular pattern.

Geeze, even without a blog to help clear her fuzzier dreams, the woolly mammoth got smitten with bright yellow buttercups still digesting.

So, carpe diem, verdad?

Yes, of course. But let's do it with some class. Let us witness some poetry crawl out of this Walmart funk hole we've born ourselves into. Use our liberal educations—read what the dead dogs wrote to become living lions once again. Don't let the consumer culture

barons fool you any longer. The woolly mammoth was a blind consumer too. What was lost in non-acquisition of petroleum plastics,
she made up for a thousand times by expressing her true nature.

Express your true nature. Become who you were before you were
born. Focus your dreams toward creative survival. Yes, even with
the weekly trade off of coins for Scott Tissue paper. Doom should
be the only preoccupation of any species' grown-up. Even the
crazed mega-neuronopolis doom of the human being king.

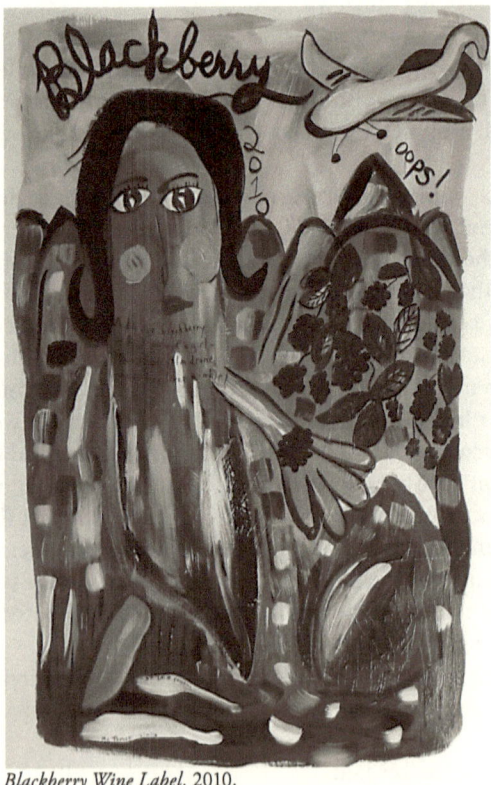

Blackberry Wine Label. 2010.
Acrylic on paper, 19 x 12"

Drone Summer

Ah, another drone summer. Droning on and on. If you are dark-skinned, financially strapped, and wielding a dry stick at the sky from behind your own countries' borders, then this is not your season. I say, Pakistani innocents of misfortune, cover your skinny brown bodies with hand-stitched mantis suits and stealth the family to Azad Kashmir. Cross over at night when the smooth bellied, vegetarian-fed Indian soldiers avoid crushing your tender insect brains for karma, and unknowingly gift their terrorized Muslim brothers a grand Hindu right-to-life.

Then the children, wives and mothers can throw off their hand-made insect disguises and convert to Nuclear Indian theocracy right away. They will be protected.

The men must press on south in your bug suits, avoiding big feet and careless boys. May I suggest leaping onto a boxcar, or a marathon rickshaw to save time? Anyway, get to the Port of Daman and stow away to work your way underground, out of sight of those killer Pentagon WASPS droning overhead.

Time will tell, but I feel your terrorized families should hide for a decade or so before arising to kill the killers.

I foretell the inevitable arrival of your own drone summer. My murderous leaders know this too. Perpetual conflict has been the policy for a couple generations, and it will carry these mortal psychos to their desired ends for perhaps one or two more.

That is the reason evil continues. It's really just mass cowardice becoming institutionalized. This is how power protects itself. For the warrior kings of any millennium, the buck never ever stops at their turn.

This generation it may. The psycho-killers can't mutilate all of your babies. Not anymore. Not with the Internet watching.

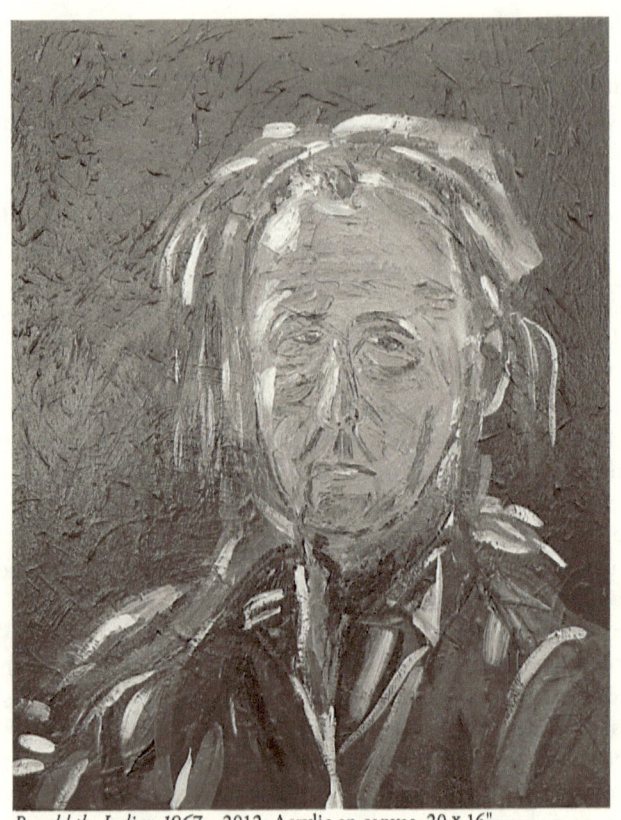

Ronald the Indian 1967–. 2012. Acrylic on canvas, 20 × 16"

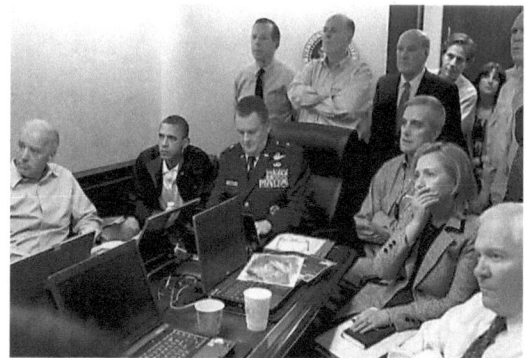

Contemporary Killer Sissies 2011

The Elder Iroquois Thinking What's Good

Here is how American chiefs watch revenge killings on television. I especially like the girl in the back on her tip toes. And the laptops. And the coffee. Our President looks like he's about to throw-up, and the brass in the middle about to pick up a cheese-burger.

These were my nation's leaders and elder statesmen, last month.
No-no. Not anymore. I have made my no-confidence vote. My children shall not obey these authorities. They have usurped power by bending tribal law. They have become a National Socialist Party holed up in a think-tank above the crematorium.
I follow Onondaga Chief Owen Lyons today. Perhaps as a child of fifty or sixty years ago, he honored and admired true braves and bravesses. Maybe the oral history of his tribe is fraught with violence and torture, unspeakable cuttings, burnings, and dis-embowelments. Sure, times could get pretty tough without toilet paper and electricity, and chiefs of the past might have handed over oversight the execution of death to the Navy Seal equivalent of their best brave swimmers in the tribe. The ones who could hold

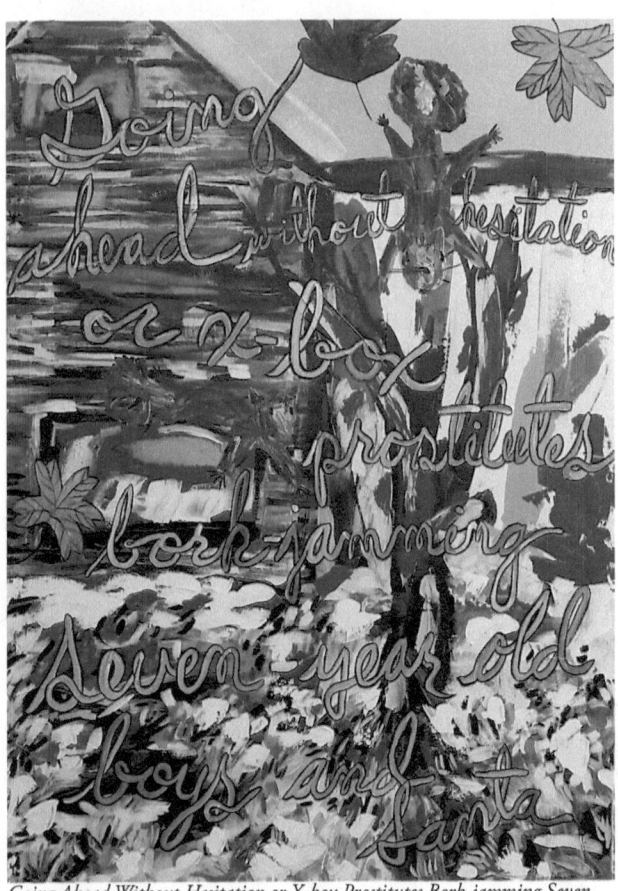

Going Ahead Without Hesitation or X-box Prostitutes Bork-jamming Seven Year Old Boys and Santa. 2013. Acrylic on canvas, 30 x 20"

their breath under water for a very, very long time... The difference (and it's a big one!) is that this real chief understood the Golden Rule was always a two-way path into the proverbial forest of dream and nightmare.

That these modern killers and torturers will ever see specific justice done to them is laughable. It will come though via more diabolical implications for the rest of the tribe.

Even the greatest cowards must confront inevitable defeat, and wake from terrifying dreams in total confusion about decisions gone horribly wrong. What truism separates the brave from the coward in any world is that the latter will take down the rest of society with him. Know this please, and teach thy children well... Each one of those criminals in the previous photo would watch our families die on television too if the enemy held them at torture-point demanding it be done.

These farcical cowards of the modern government are not the leaders of our children. We are.

Now to help our babies find chieftains who will guide them responsibly through ten thousand future sun and moons.

Ron Paul for President Please

As executive leader Ron Paul would eliminate many of the 700 U.S. bases abroad. All troops from Afghanistan, Iraq, and Libya home pronto. This is the power vested to the President. No Congress or court could stop him. To imagine that kind of money brought home is difficult. Some trillions. Everything else he espouses is interesting, but not significant. It's the war-mongering, police-state, military-industrial madness that has us all by the sneaks. The Democrans and Republicrats like Obama and Bush are bought and paid for war criminals. Dangerous, pandering puppets holding the awesome power of life and death in their soft-skin hands. America is a military state in infancy. Ron Paul would deliver a crib-death to it by the end of his first week in office. So let's not talk Medicare and abortion and gun control blah-blah-blah. A president has no real power over any of these wedge issues anyway. Even his court nominees must be confirmed by both parties. We can use our Constitution and improve its worth to be more than the paper it was written on. Let's just use it for once when it matters most.

Maybe what our citizens need is some time for night school and a civics lesson.

Remember, as president, Paul would limit his own powers to the Constitution. Has anyone read it? It used to be the law. Now presidents declare the executive right to bomb Libya, Pakistan, Yemen, who knows where else?—that means make war on other nations without congressional approval. If Ron Paul is an acolyte of Ayn Rand, and named the Junior senator from Kentucky after Daddy's favorite novelist, then I believe our last three presidents, had they baby boys, would Christen them Beelzebub, Prince of Darkness, and Satan respectively. There are millions of Pakistani, Afghan, Iraqi, Yemeni, and Libyan people who would agree.

Seriously though, neither Paul, nor anyone else, becomes God if elected President. Yet at least with Paul we could be assured of a respectable civilian at the helm. And from that power podium, he would end this world-encompassing military madness. It might behoove us all to rethink how a humble conservative congressman from Texas could fix an inflated economy with an order to shut down the Empire's military bases all over the globe. All troops home immediately. So much life and money spared. Also, no more TSA, no Homeland Security—the latter being some psychotic "Vaterland" dream out of fascist Cheney's scary brain. Hooray! No more Patriot Act, no more 1984 groupthink realized...

Paul is the only peace candidate in today's topsy-turvy world of anti-morality.

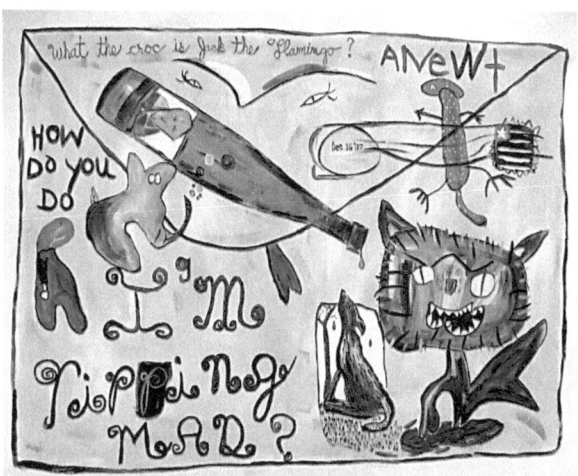

How Do You Do I'm Ripping Mad? 2007.
Acrylic on paper, 15 x 22"

Argument for Torture

"We must torture our own to protect us from them." Them. And them. Them too. And these guys.

Oh boy, these scary Muslims are gonna come get us on their donkeys! Watch out! Run!

Some of us are old enough to remember Gorbachev's nasty head rash. Wasn't it so scary? Stallone and Reagan longed to video bomb a hundred of his nation's kids into oblivion in secret too. Just technology lagged behind their sadistic hopes and dreams. So they made movie propaganda and resorted to traditional, manned, torture methods in secret cement block buildings around the world.

Obama, Bush, Clinton, Bush Senior, Reagan melt-skin—They are the Hitlers and Stalins of future world history. Watch out Islews of the East, the "dronocaust" is in full swing.

Make suffer a thousand families. Break down their modesty to the point of goading a once very shy, unobtrusive mother, into ex-

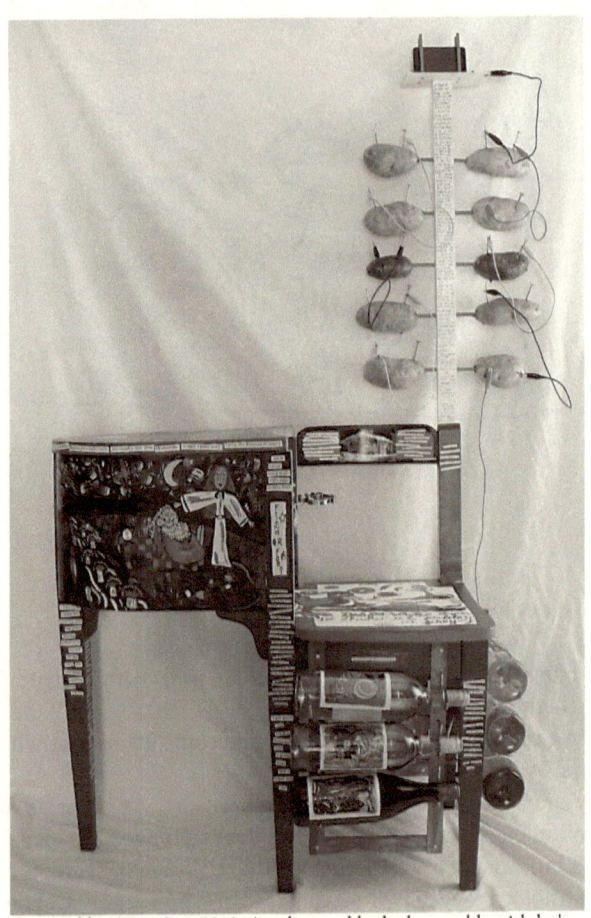

Armageddon Wine Bar. 2010. Acrylic on old telephone table with lot's of homemade wine, potatoes and a movie, 60 × 26 × 21"

ploding her insides out at the city market. We have been made to
fear her. She is the new Brezhnev. She, and all of her evil kind will
"bury" us. Of course not until she can equip her families' Chinese
made Changan Kalam van to swim, or fly unmanned, launching
missiles with stolen Lockheed Martin technology.

No, enraged Muslims of earth do not frighten me. I am terrified
of the psych-op eyeballs of my immediate neighbors. Anytime I
see the big screen on, while I voyeur about the neighborhood and
pass by the 40-something, sagging joggers, I hope and pray for a
foreign people strong enough to drone our diseased complacency
away for good. I long for a post-WWII Germanic depression and
guilt to inflict the minds of our retarded people.

How I long for a humble neighbor!

Come to the Wine Bar and Despair Over a Pretend Good Time

It's run on potatoes!

The military has lost all credibility. So has government and
God in church. Our conquistadors don't want gold, or even mass
conversions to run off the charts. These Kansas-Nebraska psychos
just want to watch little kids die. There are no ministers, priests,
rabbis, or mullahs twittering a moral philosophy. No privates fresh
out of training, realizing the madness, and fragging their keepers.
Like the rosy-cheeked people of Ballstedt, Germany, celebrating
Christmas a mile from the curious roasting smells of Buchenwald,
we heartless zombies of Anytown, America pretend glee, while
ignoring instant messages of mass murder by national representa-
tives of our own flesh and blood. No, we cannot smell the charred
remains of some seven-year-old Afghan boys picking up sticks on
a mountainside. And we might live a happy day or two longer for
it. Unlike the Germans of Ballstedt, however, enjoying the fruits
of many battles won while toasting the helpless, Americans will
lose their Children's Crusade by internal means, not a minute after
their dollar compresses into the purchasing power of a Weimar
penny.

For those of you who at least wince upon hearing news of war
crimes, stop by the wine bar for an aperitif, and we'll share a hot
potato before bedtime.

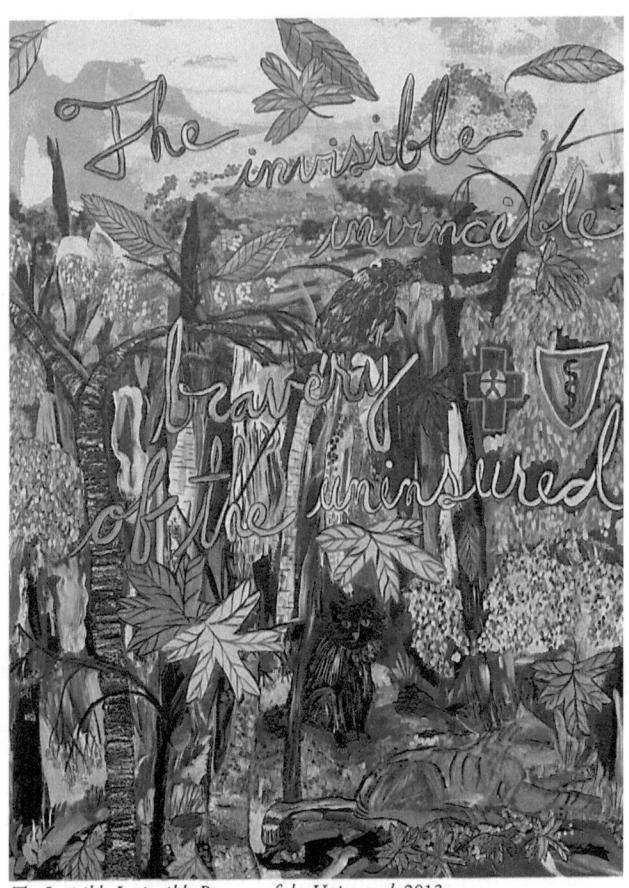

The Invisible Invincible Bravery of the Uninsured. 2013.
Acrylic on canvas, 48 x 36"

The Invisible Economy

An across-the-board 50% cut in income for Americans, and this place would erupt into a 300 million human MadMax nightmare.

We should thank our lucky stars that the powerful are holding up the ceiling, for now anyway.

When it does give way, our commissioned military police won't be so well-behaved as their Egyptian counterparts. Excepting the majority of children, this nation is united by a psychological conglomeration of fear, avarice, and more fear.

In human history, mass super-comfort has yet to maintain any lasting communion. We are a nation of entitled "little emperors," delusional feudal lords dreaming about Facebook crusades and Twitter accolades, while the lowly of earth, who have subsisted over the years on grass and grubs, discover an immense power of brotherhood using the same state-of-the-art technological tools for dreaming.

I am monarch of all I survey
My right there is none to dispute

Thanks William Cowper for your fake nature wig!
Thank you Henry Thoreau for spreading your Mrs. Emerson feed me individualism.

The 19th century could have ended with an empathetic Dickens mentality, but here in America, finished with the dandy entitlement dreams of a coddled Teddy Roosevelt.

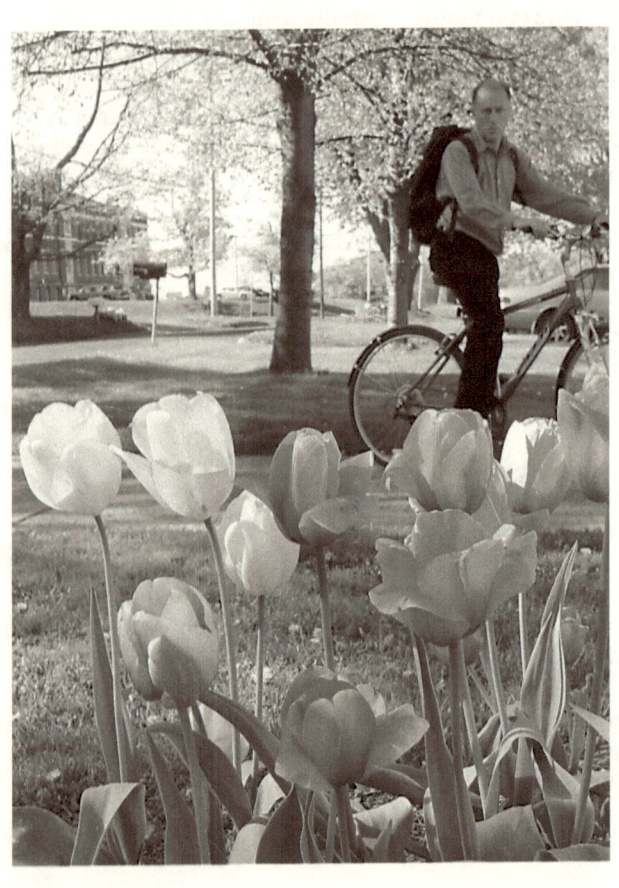

Finally, I Am Rich Beyond Other People's Wildest Dreams

Here's me, riding off to a solo show in mid-May.

The tulips can be Amsterdam or Paris. I could be the wealthiest acrylic entrepreneur on planet earth, and am, whether the banker believes me or not. I have decided that it is all about perception. So this morning, on our first floor balcony, overlooking the soft greens of this ancient American paradise, I shall opt to increase the income of my career-lie a thousandfold.

See the mid-forty year old above, with his bike ride and back-pack? He doesn't need anymore phony dimes because he is already stinking rich.

Free from disease, broad-shouldered, even quite handsome from a distance, I mimic the last American bike-rider of taste. I am the Henry Miller I dreamed about becoming as a boy. I am pedaling my bike out to the burbs of Paris on a Saturday afternoon musing about wine and cheese that I cannot afford. I inhale powerful drafts of dinosaur breath. The great dead ones survive in me. I carry on exactly what their lives lived me to.

Fantastic.

Oswego, N.Y. December, 2013.